Best Easy Day Hikes Series

Best Easy Day Hikes
Yosemite
National Park

Fifth Edition

Suzanne Swedo

FALCONGUIDES

GUILFORD, CONNECTICUT

FALCONGUIDES®

An imprint of The Rowman & Littlefield Publishing Group, Inc.
4501 Forbes Blvd., Ste. 200
Lanham, MD 20706
www.rowman.com
Falcon and FalconGuides are registered trademarks and Make
Adventure Your Story is a trademark of The Rowman & Littlefield
Publishing Group, Inc.

Distributed by NATIONAL BOOK NETWORK

British Library Cataloguing in Publication Information available

Library of Congress Cataloging-in-Publication Data available

ISBN 978-1-4930-4033-9 (paperback)
ISBN 978-1-4930-4034-6 (e-book)

∞™ The paper used in this publication meets the minimum
requirements of American National Standard for Information
Sciences—Permanence of Paper for Printed Library Materials, ANSI/
NISO Z39.48-1992.

Printed in the United States of America

For Mom

Contents

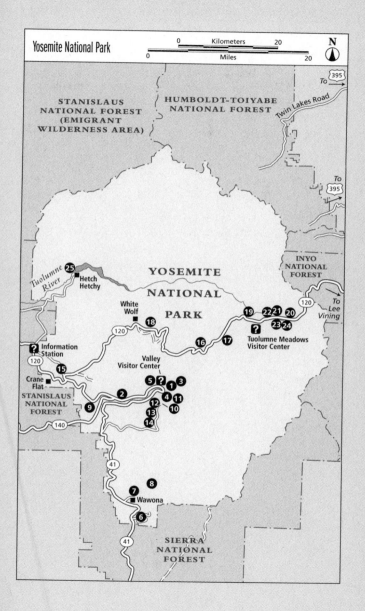

Yosemite National Park

STANISLAUS
NATIONAL FOREST
(EMIGRANT
WILDERNESS AREA)

HUMBOLDT-TOIYABE
NATIONAL FOREST

Twin Lakes Road

To 395

To 395

INYO
NATIONAL
FOREST

YOSEMITE

NATIONAL

PARK

Tuolumne River

25 Hetch Hetchy

White Wolf

18

120

19 22 21 20
23 24

120

To Lee Vining

Information Station

120

15

Crane Flat

STANISLAUS
NATIONAL
FOREST

140

9

2

16   17

Tuolumne Meadows
Visitor Center

Valley
Visitor Center

5 1 3

4 11

10

12
13
14

41

8

7 Wawona

6

41

SIERRA
NATIONAL
FOREST

Acknowledgments

Thanks to the National Park Service, especially Ranger Mark Fincher, whose suggestions and advice were invaluable. Thanks also to the personnel and volunteers of the Yosemite Conservancy.

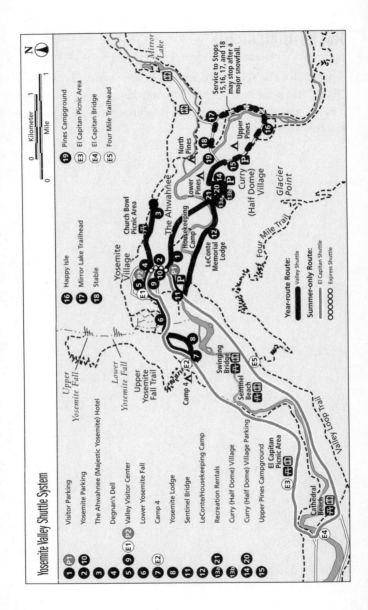

Yosemite Valley Shuttle System

1 P1 Visitor Parking
2 **10** Yosemite Parking
3 The Ahwahnee (Majestic Yosemite) Hotel
4 Degnan's Deli
5 **9** E1 P2 Valley Visitor Center
6 Lower Yosemite Fall
7 E2 Camp 4
8 Yosemite Lodge
11 Sentinel Bridge
12 LeConte/Housekeeping Camp
13a **21** Recreation Rentals
13b Curry (Half Dome) Village
14 **20** Curry (Half Dome) Village Parking
15 Upper Pines Campground

16 Happy Isle
17 Mirror Lake Trailhead
18 Stable
19 Pines Campground
E3 El Capitan Picnic Area
E4 El Capitan Bridge
E5 Four Mile Trailhead

Service to Stops 15, 16, 17, and 18 may stop after a major snowfall.

Year-route Route:
Valley Shuttle

Summer-only Route:
El Capitan Shuttle
Express Shuttle

Introduction

This book is for a great many of the nearly five million visitors to Yosemite National Park each year who have a limited amount of time to spend but want to sample some of the best features of the park on foot. Yosemite's borders encompass almost 1,200 square miles in east-central California, though the majority of tourists congregate in Yosemite Valley and miss much of the spectacular wild country beyond. The hikes described here are scattered throughout the entire park. All are accessible by paved roads, and none is difficult to find.

The hikes vary in length, but none is longer than 5 miles. The shorter hikes are not necessarily the easier ones. Because this is rugged country with few level places, most hikes do involve a little elevation gain and loss. Use the list of hikes ranked in order of difficulty to make your choice. All are on clearly marked, easy-to-follow trails.

Leave No Trace

The trails that weave through Yosemite National Park are heavily used and take a real beating, but staying on trails leaves the least impact on the land Hikers can do their part by respecting park rules and practicing Leave No Trace principles (LNT.org). Official trails are built to retard erosion as well as to create a more comfortable (and safer) grade for gaining and losing elevation. To prevent damage to trails please do not shortcut switchbacks.

Among the most important and obvious rules for day hikers: Please don't litter. ORANGE PEELS ARE LITTER!

Please do not leave your used toilet paper in the wilderness for others to find. Carry a small plastic bag with you to pack it out.

1

For Your Safety

Things not to worry about:

Bears: Nobody has ever been killed by a bear in Yosemite (though there have been two deaths caused by mule deer). Yosemite bears are afraid of humans. When you meet one in a populated area, maintain our fierce reputation by hollering, waving your arms, and looking ferocious. When you meet a bear on the trail, make some noise so that you don't take it by surprise; once it is aware of you, the two of you can continue on your separate ways.

Things to be aware of, though not to worry about:

Water: The leading cause of accidental death in Yosemite is traffic accidents. The leading cause of accidental death in the Yosemite *wilderness* is drowning. Hikers consistently underestimate the depth and power of water in rivers and streams. A few have ignored signs warning about swimming or wading in especially dangerous spots—and died as a result.

Be Prepared

Carry a basic first-aid kit, rain gear, a flashlight, snacks, and a map. Carry plenty of water with you. Sierra streams look clean and clear, but they may contain microorganisms that can make you sick. Do not drink water from streams or other natural water sources without purifying it.

Notes about Name Changes

Since the park has changed concessionaires, there have been some controversial changes of the names of commercial properties and locations. Many longtime Yosemite visitors still think of the original names as the "real" ones and continue to use them. (Of course the names Yosemite's Native American people used here were the truly original ones.) The older names are also found on earlier park maps and publications. This can be confusing to people coming to Yosemite for the first time, so here are a few of the changes you are most likely to encounter:

Old Name	New Name
The Ahwahnee Hotel	The Majestic Yosemite Hotel
Curry Village	Half Dome Village
The Wawona Hotel	The Big Trees Lodge
Badger Pass	Yosemite Ski and Snowboard Area

Ranking the Hikes

The following list ranks the hikes in this book from easiest to most challenging.

Easiest

Most Challenging

Map Legend

395	US Highway
120	State Highway
	Local/Park Road
	Unpaved Road
	Featured Trail
	Trail
	Boardwalk
	River/Creek
	Intermittent Creek
	Body of Water
	Intermittent Lake
	Marsh/Swamp
	Escarpment
	National Park/Forest
	Bridge
	Camping
	Gate
	Nature Trail
	Parking
	Peak
	Picnic Area
	Point of Interest/Structure
	Ranger Station
	Restrooms
	Spring
	Trailhead
	Viewpoint/Overlook
	Visitor/Information Center
	Waterfall

Yosemite Valley

Yosemite Valley is one of the natural wonders of the world. Almost-vertical walls rise more than 4,700 feet above the valley floor, where the Merced River winds its way through flower-filled meadows and shady forests. The famous profile of Half Dome dominates the east end; El Capitan, the west. Some of the world's highest waterfalls pour from the cliffs. It's a mecca for hikers, climbers, photographers, anglers, rafters, cyclists, and just plain tourists from every place on Earth.

Although the valley covers only about 7 square miles of a national park that sprawls over 1,200 square miles, the valley is where the majority of visitors stay. Indeed, many believe that Yosemite Valley and Yosemite National Park are one and the same. Do not expect a wilderness experience in the valley, but don't assume that hiking there is not worthwhile just because it's popular. There are many beautiful, quiet, out-of-the-way corners to enjoy on foot and in solitude, especially if you have done some planning.

Yosemite Valley has become so popular it can be a source of aggravation instead of joy when you first arrive, stuck in your car on a hot afternoon moving at about the same pace as you would in one of the world's bigger cities at rush hour. Do not expect to drive in and find a room or a campsite, though occasionally, if your karma is good, you might score a last-minute vacancy or cancellation. Accommodations are limited in the valley, indeed, in the whole park. Make overnight reservations as far in advance as possible.

If you are passing through, or plan to spend only a day in Yosemite Valley, arrive as early in the morning as possible, head to one of the main day-use parking areas, park there, and walk or ride the free shuttle bus that goes to most trailheads. There may be lines to enter the park from any of the entrance kiosks, and once you have reached the valley, parking lots may be full.

If you're out on the trail before 9 a.m., the valley floor will be yours to explore and enjoy. By midday, however, you will be joining the crowds, craning your neck to see the scenery or waiting in line for a snack or for information at the visitor center.

Contact Yosemite National Park at (209) 372-0200 or visit the park's website (nps.gov/yose) for more information in advance of your visit.

1 East Valley Floor

This flat hike, partly along the Merced River, passes through forests, meadows, and a swampy fen with views of North Dome and Yosemite Falls. Along the way, you can visit the Happy Isles Art and Nature Center and the site of a notorious rockslide.

Distance: 2.2-mile loop
Elevation change: Minimal
Hiking time: 1–3 hours
Trail surface: Paved path, board-walk, and forest floor
Difficulty: Easy

Map: USGS Half Dome
Best time to go: Year-round
Facilities: Food, supplies, phones, restrooms, and water at Half Dome (Curry) Village

Finding the trailhead: Board the Yosemite Valley shuttle bus from anyplace in the valley and get off at Stop 15, Upper Pines, and continue walking along the shuttle bus road in the same direction for 0.1 mile to the hikers' parking lot on the right. If you are driving, follow Southside Drive to the east end of the valley. Pass Half Dome (Curry) Village and follow the signs to the trailhead parking sign. Turn right into the hikers' parking lot. The trailhead is at the far east end of the lot. There are plenty of boxes for you to store your food out of the reach of bears, but there are no restrooms and no water at the trailhead. (Both are available at Happy Isles.)

Please do not leave trash in the bear-proof boxes. GPS: N37 44.10' / W119 33.97'

The Hike

From the trailhead sign marking the John Muir and Mist Trails, follow the wide, obvious path straight ahead into the shady ponderosa pine and incense cedar forest. You will notice another log-lined path cutting off from this one to the left, heading back to the shuttle bus road, but the right-hand path is prettier and quieter.

Pass a little A-frame structure used for ranger/naturalist talks and soon find yourself clomping across a boardwalk through a swampy area known as The Fen. It's filled with a dense growth of water-loving horsetails, sedges, and fragrant mint and is a great place to spot, or just listen to, birds. At the end of the boardwalk, the trail meets a paved path where a sign points to the left (north) for the John Muir Trail and to the right (south) to the Happy Isles Art and Nature Center (open in summer only). Consider a short detour to see the exhibits and books inside, then walk around to the back for a view of the rubble and smashed trees left by the deadly 1996 rockfall. An interpretive sign notes that such events are fairly common in Yosemite.

From the Art and Nature Center, backtrack to the north (downstream) and follow the path along the Merced River to shuttle bus Stop 16 for Happy Isles. There are restrooms and water here. Turn right onto the shuttle bus road and cross the bridge over the river. Be sure to pause on the bridge for the view to the left (downstream) of North Dome with the river in the foreground, a photographers' favorite. Cross the road, turn left, and leave most of the noise and people behind. Follow a path of incense cedars and pines, streamside alders, and dogwoods along the Merced. Showy white azaleas perfume the air in May and June. The river changes character at every turn—sometimes gurgling green and placid, sometimes rushing noisily around wooded islands.

At 1.9 miles you pass the stable area (the horses have been moved to Wawona) and Upper Yosemite Falls comes into

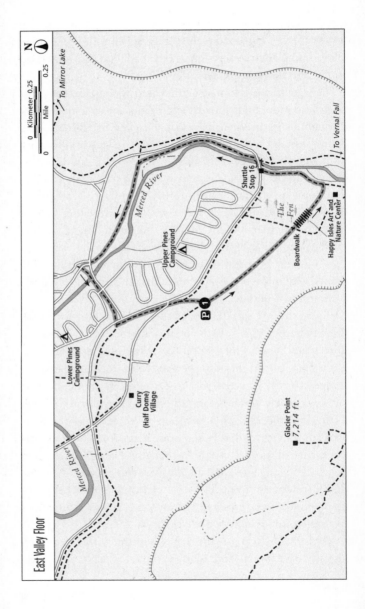

East Valley Floor

Merced River

Merced River

To Mirror Lake

To Vernal Fall

Lower Pines Campground

Upper Pines Campground

Curry (Half Dome) Village

Shuttle Stop 16

The Fen

Boardwalk

Happy Isles Art and Nature Center

Glacier Point 7,214 ft.

P 1

N

0 Kilometer 0.25

0 Mile 0.25

view ahead. Turn left to cross the Clark Bridge back over the Merced, and keep to the trail on the right side of the road to avoid traffic. Pass between the entrances to Upper Pines and Lower Pines Campgrounds. The white tent cabins of Curry (Half Dome) Village appear across Southside Drive. Turn left at the T intersection and follow the shuttle bus road past Stop 15 again to find the hikers' parking lot on the right.

Miles and Directions

0.0 Start at the trailhead at the hikers' parking lot.

0.8 Cross The Fen on a boardwalk.

0.9 Pass Happy Isles Art and Nature Center.

1.0 Cross the Happy Isles bridge over the Merced.

1.9 Turn left at the site of the old stables.

2.1 Reach Southside Drive; turn left.

2.2 Arrive back at the trailhead.

2 West Valley Floor

This is a longer hike, but there is little elevation change. Start early, take a picnic, and make a day of it. Along the way are opportunities for swimming or wading, good places to watch the climbers on the face of El Capitan, and fine views of several famous waterfalls in spring and early summer. The falls are mostly dry by mid–August, and the valley floor can be hot in summer, but most of the trail is in the shade.

Distance: 4.7-mile loop
Elevation change: Minimal
Hiking time: 2–4 hours
Trail surface: Paved path and forest floor
Difficulty: Moderately easy
Maps: USGS El Capitan, Half Dome

Best time to go: Spring through fall
Facilities: Food, water, and restrooms at Yosemite Lodge; restrooms at Valley View and Bridalveil Fall

Finding the trailhead: From CA 120 and CA 140, cross the one-way Pohono Drive to Southside Drive. Curve around the west end of the valley and continue on Southside Drive, passing Bridalveil Fall. Then turn left (northwest) onto the El Capitan Bridge. Park on the far (west) end of the bridge.

From CA 41, after entering the valley through the Wawona Tunnel, stay on Southside Drive, passing Bridalveil Fall to the El Capitan Bridge road; turn left onto the bridge. Park on the far (west) end of the bridge. If you arrive early enough, you should find a parking space along the road.

In summer only, you can take the El Capitan shuttle bus from Yosemite Village all the way to Stop E-4. GPS: N37 43.45' / W119 37.88'

The Hike

From the west end of the El Capitan Bridge spanning the Merced River, turn right (north) and set off upstream on the path between the river and Northside Drive. The trail sign at the start says "Pohono Bridge 2.8 miles." You can't miss the 7,569-foot monolith of El Capitan directly ahead, while Cathedral Rocks and Cathedral Spires rise behind you. Skirt a low fence blocking access to the river as it rounds a curve called the Devil's Elbow. Cross Northside Drive at the crosswalk and make a sharp hairpin turn back westward along an old gravel road. The formidable North American Wall of El Capitan looms directly overhead. The wall is a patch of darker-colored mineral in the granite shaped like the North American continent.

You will probably be close enough to see figures clinging to the rock above even without binoculars and might hear their shouted conversations. As you approach The Nose of El Cap, you cross several spur routes used by climbers to reach the base of the wall. If it's early in the season, you will probably have to hop across several branches of Ribbon Creek as it flows down the cliff, and you can get a rare view of this 1,612-foot-high waterfall that dissolves into a mist near the bottom and is usually entirely dry by late June.

Your route soon reaches the Old Big Oak Flat Road, where you turn left and in just a few steps find the trail again on your right. Follow it beneath the fire-blackened trunks of trees until you descend almost all the way down to Northside Drive, where you can see Bridalveil Fall, though there is a better view ahead (as well as a restroom). Veer right (north) away from the road for a time and pass around the back side of Black Spring through a riotous growth of willows, cattails, horsetails, and ferns.

The trail angles back down toward the road again, where you will be able to spot cars parked at Valley View, one of the classic postcard portraits of Bridalveil Fall at mile 2.6. Continue westward and in a few minutes reach a crosswalk across Northside Drive, then cross over the Merced on the Pohono Bridge at mile 2.8. Just past the bridge a sign says "Bridalveil Fall 1.6 miles." This is a lovely, quiet corner of the valley where dogwoods bloom in spring and maples glow red in fall. There are two little springs across the road, Fern Spring and Moss Spring. This section of the trail can be muddy in springtime, but it hosts a garden of flowers with evocative names like enchanter's nightshade and bleeding heart. The trail hugs the riverside for a time then emerges into sunshine, skirting Bridalveil Meadow. Across Southside Drive, a sign marks the site of the famous confab between John Muir and Teddy Roosevelt about the importance of protecting places like Yosemite in a national park system.

The "official" trail stays to the left of the road and crosses several branches of Bridalveil Creek, but unless it's very late in the season, you'll stay dryer and safer if you leave the trail and walk along the shoulder of the road. At this point Southside Drive, the Wawona Road, and CA 41 come together, so watch the traffic. You will have to backtrack just a few feet on CA 41 to visit Bridalveil Fall at mile 4.3, which flows over the southern wall of Yosemite through a defile between Cathedral Rocks and the Leaning Tower. Before the fall reaches the valley floor 620 feet below, the wind catches, tatters, and flings the droplets into lacy patterns of spray.

Leave Bridalveil Fall on a wide path and continue eastward, parallel to Southside Drive. Turn right at a junction

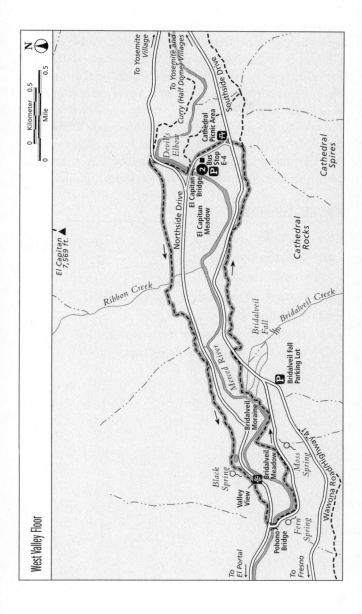

West Valley Floor

directing you to Curry (Half Dome) Village and climb over the hump of the Bridalveil Moraine amid a tumble of enormous mossy rocks. Once the trail flattens out, watch the right side of the trail for a low post with a picture of a carabiner, which marks a route for climbers. A few yards beyond, at a second carabiner sign at mile 4.7, find an unmarked but clear trail leading left out of the forest to Southside Drive. Turn right here and in only a few steps find yourself at the junction with the road over El Capitan Bridge; turn sharply left here and follow the road back to your starting point.

Miles and Directions

0.0   Start at El Capitan Bridge.

0.3   Cross Northside Drive.

2.7   Come to Valley View.

2.8   Cross the Pohono Bridge.

4.3   Reach Bridalveil Fall.

4.6   Turn right onto an unmarked trail to Southside Drive.

4.7   Turn left and arrive back at the trailhead.

3 Vernal Fall View

This popular hike follows the first mile of the famous John Muir Trail along the roaring Merced River to where Vernal Fall plunges down the final step of the Giant Staircase. Don't expect a true wilderness experience here. This is probably the most heavily used route out of Yosemite Valley. The way is steadily uphill, but the trail is short, mostly paved, and well worth the effort.

Distance: 1.6 miles out and back
Elevation gain: 400 feet
Hiking time: 1–3 hours
Trail surface: Paved
Difficulty: Moderate
Map: USGS Half Dome

Best time to go: Spring through fall
Facilities: Snack bar, water, toilets, and phones at Happy Isles; water and toilets at the Vernal Fall Bridge

Finding the trailhead: Board the Yosemite Valley shuttle bus from anywhere in the valley and get off at Stop 16, Happy Isles. If you are driving, you can park in the trailhead parking lot just east of Curry Village, though it is often full. There are bear-proof boxes where you can leave food and ice chests. You will have to walk to Happy Isles from here, adding 0.8 mile round-trip to your hike. GPS: N37 43.57' / W119 33.31'

The Hike

The Merced River first plunges over the steps of the Giant Staircase as Nevada Fall, then as Vernal Fall, before it slows to sweeping meanders over the flat floor of Yosemite Valley.

If time permits, hike or drive up to Glacier Point for a spectacular overhead view of the Giant Staircase.

Happy Isles is the site of the notorious rockfall of 1996. To see the devastation up close, make a short detour to the Happy Isles Nature Center, just upstream from the shuttle stop. Cross the Happy Isles Bridge over the Merced. When you are almost all the way to the other side, pause and look to your left (downstream) for a great view of North Dome, a photographers' favorite. Once across the river, turn right (south) at a sign indicating the Mist Trail, Vernal Fall, Nevada Fall, and the John Muir Trail. Follow the broad, usually very busy path that skirts the eastern shore of the river for 0.1 mile, where the trail narrows and turns left (west) into the forest. A short distance ahead, a huge sign marks the beginning of the John Muir Trail. The sign shows mileage to various points along the way to trail's end at Mount Whitney, 211 miles to the south.

The trail climbs through black oak and pine forest among enormous lichen-draped boulders above the east bank of the Merced. A little spring trickles out of the rocks a few hundred yards up on your left. (*Caution:* Don't drink the water without purifying it.) The trail steepens gradually as you climb, but you will want to stop frequently anyway to enjoy the roaring river through openings in the trees. After about 0.5 mile look across the Merced to your right (south). Tucked back up in Illilouette Gorge, Illilouette Falls pours 370 feet down the Panorama Cliff to meet the Merced River. Most people miss it. Glance behind you now and then to find that Upper Yosemite Falls is visible too.

The trail descends to the bridge at 0.8 mile, where dozens of visitors will be taking photos or staring in open-mouthed wonder at 317-foot Vernal Fall. There are restrooms nearby,

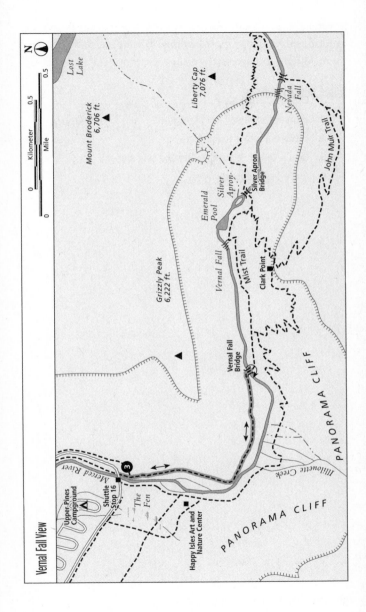

Vernal Fall View

N

Lost Lake

Mount Broderick
6,706 ft. ▲

Liberty Cap
7,076 ft. ▲

Kilometer 0.5

Mile 0.5

Grizzly Peak
6,222 ft. ▲

Emerald Pool

Silver Apron

Nevada Fall

Vernal Fall

Mist Trail

Silver Apron Bridge

Vernal Fall Bridge

▲

Clark Point

John Muir Trail

PANORAMA CLIFF

Merced River

Upper Pines Campground

Shuttle Stop 16

3

The Fen

Illilouette Creek

Happy Isles Art and Nature Center

PANORAMA CLIFF

a water fountain, and dozens of freeloading Steller's jays and ground squirrels. For their health and your safety, do not feed them. When you are ready, return the way you came.

Miles and Directions

0.0   Start at the Happy Isles trailhead.

0.5   Views open to Illilouette Fall.

0.8   Reach Vernal Fall Bridge. Retrace your steps.

1.6   Arrive back at Happy Isles.

4 Mirror Lake

The walk to Mirror Lake is a family favorite offering little beaches and shallow water to splash in during summer, classic reflection for photographers in spring, and plenty of birds in the surrounding willows.

Distance: 2.0 miles out and back
Elevation change: 100 feet
Hiking time: 1–2 hours
Trail surface: Part abandoned road, part forest floor
Difficulty: Easy
Map: USGS Half Dome

Best time to go: Year-round; best in May and June, when the dogwood is in bloom and the water level is high enough for Mount Watkins to cast the reflection that gives the lake its name
Facilities: Restrooms; no potable water

Finding the trailhead: Board the Yosemite Valley shuttle bus from anyplace in the valley and get off at Stop 17, Mirror Lake. The nearest parking lot with a shuttle bus stop is at Curry Village. GPS: N37 44.22' / W119 33.35'

The Hike

Mirror Lake was created when a rockslide dammed up a section of Tenaya Creek, which promptly went to work to reclaim its original course. Every spring it washes tons of silt down the canyon to refill the lake basin, extending fingers of earth into the water. This in turn invites colonization by water-loving plants like sedges and willows, which soon come alive with the songs of red-winged blackbirds.

Mirror Lake is well on its way to becoming Mirror Meadow. Eventually, as the basin fills in and dries out, the area may become forest with Tenaya Creek running through it, someday leaving the canyon as though Mirror Lake had never been—at least until the next major rockslide. A smaller, more recent rockfall occurred in March 2009 when Ahwiyah Point, the pointed projection just to the left (east) of Half Dome, dropped many tons of rock 1,800 feet, blocking the trail on the opposite side of Mirror Lake for several years. (It has since been rebuilt.) The best view is from your side, however. Look for the fresh, light-colored scars on the rock face.

For years the park service periodically dredged the lake, slowing the natural succession from lake to forest in order to preserve the popular reflection, but the practice was finally discontinued. Interpretive exhibits along the way help visitors appreciate the way the natural world continually transforms itself.

From the shuttle bus stop, the sign for Mirror Lake points you along the paved road (no longer in use except for bicycles) to the Tenaya Creek Bridge. Just before you cross the bridge a wide dirt path cuts off to the right (east) to follow the eastern shore of the river and the lake; your route keeps left and crosses the bridge. Beyond, the path splits again. The path to the left is dirt trail; the road is the more scenic route, since it follows the creek.

Both road and trail rise slightly, passing through a quiet forest of ponderosa pine, white fir, Douglas fir, incense cedar, and dogwood. At 1.0 mile the forest opens to reveal tranquil Mirror Lake, reflecting Mount Watkins. Half Dome rises abruptly to the east.

There are sandy beaches along the lakeshore for picnics and wading. Return the way you came.

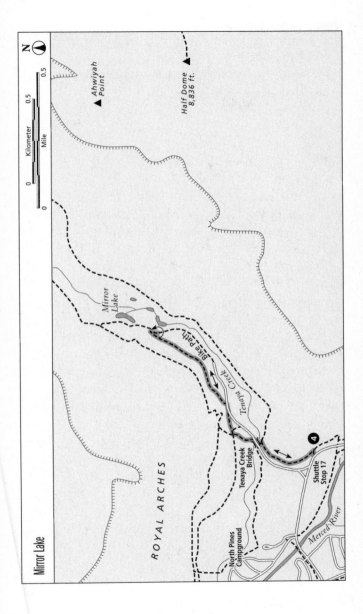

Mirror Lake

ROYAL ARCHES

Mirror Lake

Bike Path

Tenaya Creek

Tenaya Creek Bridge

North Pines Campground

Shuttle Stop 17

Merced River

Ahwiyah Point

Half Dome
8,836 ft.

N

0   0.5   Kilometer
0   0.5   Mile

Miles and Directions

0.0   Start at the Mirror Lake trailhead.

1.0   Reach the shore of Mirror Lake. Retrace your steps.

2.0   Arrive back at the trailhead.

5 Yosemite Falls

Yosemite Falls is among the most famous and frequently photographed falls in the world, and this walk gives you the closest top-to-bottom head-on view you can get anywhere. The trail crosses a bridge so close to the base of the lowest fall that you can feel the spray early in the season. This hike is more dramatic when done clockwise.

Distance: 0.7-mile loop
Elevation change: Minimal
Hiking time: About 1 hour
Trail surface: Paved path, boardwalk, and forest floor
Difficulty: Easy
Maps: USGS Half Dome, Yosemite Falls

Best time to go: Year-round, but best Nov to mid-Aug. The falls are dry late summer and early fall.
Facilities: Toilets and picnic area at the trailhead; food and supplies available at Yosemite Lodge

Finding the trailhead: Ride the Yosemite Valley shuttle bus from anywhere in the valley to Stop 7. GPS: N37 44.74' / W119 35.61'

The Hike

According to some, this is the highest waterfall (2,425 feet) on the continent. It is actually a series of three falls—the upper one dropping 1,430 feet, a middle series of cascades totaling 675 feet, and a lower one tumbling 320 feet—and qualifies as the highest only if all three are added together. In May and June, the thunder of the water from melting snow falling onto the rocks below can be heard all over the valley, and the spray drenches onlookers many yards away. On full-moon nights in May, visitors may see the famous

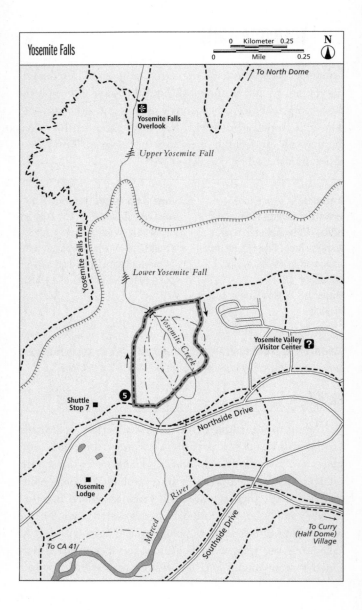

Yosemite Falls

0 — Kilometer — 0.25
0 — Mile — 0.25

N

To North Dome

Yosemite Falls Overlook

Upper Yosemite Fall

Yosemite Falls Trail

Lower Yosemite Fall

Yosemite Creek

Yosemite Valley Visitor Center

Shuttle Stop 7

5

Northside Drive

Yosemite Lodge

Merced River

Southside Drive

To CA 41

To Curry (Half Dome) Village

"moonbow" first described by John Muir. The volume decreases as the summer wears on, and by September the falls are completely dry. In winter the frozen spray forms an eerie ice cone at the base.

From the shuttle bus stop you will see a path heading directly north; instead, turn left (west) and follow the path parallel to the road for about 100 yards until you see the restrooms. Turn right (south) at the big sign.

The big red trees you notice as you first get off the shuttle are not redwoods or sequoias but incense cedars; they may smell like the yellow pencils you used in school. The trail winds almost imperceptibly uphill through the forest toward the base of the falls to a wide viewing area and a bridge. At several points along the route are turnouts with interpretive panels about the human and natural history of the area that are well worth pausing to read. The bridge crosses the creek very near the base of the cliff. If it is early spring, you're sure to be dampened by the spray.

Despite posted warning signs, the huge slippery boulders are usually crawling with people. Beyond the bridge, the trail follows along the base of the cliff and then swings south behind some park employee housing. It winds through braided strands of the now-divided creek and then curves again to meet Northside Drive near the shuttle stop.

Miles and Directions

0.0 Start at the Yosemite Falls trailhead.

0.3 Cross the bridge at Lower Yosemite Fall.

0.7 Arrive back at the trailhead.

Wawona and the Southern Park

The trails into the southern park begin from Wawona, the short spur road off CA 41 to the Mariposa Grove of Big Trees, or the Foresta Road off CA 120. Most trailheads start at around 4,000 feet and offer hiking opportunities earlier in the season than in other parts of Yosemite. You'll find more solitude in this part of the park too, because there is less water in high summer, the time when most people visit Yosemite, though the Mariposa Grove of giant sequoias is always busy. The Mariposa Grove lies just inside the south entrance of the park. Wawona, about 4 miles inside the park, is the site of a historic overnight stage stop on the way to Yosemite Valley, with a small grocery, gift shop, visitor center, and gas station. The beautiful old Wawona Hotel, now known as the Big Trees Lodge, built in the 1870s, is still in operation, along with a historic pioneer town, stables, and even a golf course.

Just past "town," a new bridge crosses the Merced River. Just past that, Chilnualna Falls Road, on the right, leads through the little settlement of North Wawona, a private inholding.

6 Grizzly Giant and the Mariposa Grove

The giant sequoias are the largest living things on Earth, and, enduring more than 2,000 years, they are also among the oldest. The bristlecone pines in the White Mountains to the east are older, and the coast redwoods are taller, but these are certainly the most massive and most awe-inspiring of the big trees. This is the largest of Yosemite's three sequoia groves, with more than 500 of the big trees. The Mariposa Grove is the most popular, and the Grizzly Giant—your main objective—is the largest living tree in any of the groves.

The newly restored Mariposa Grove reopened in June 2018 following completion of a project financed in partnership with the Yosemite Conservancy and begun in 2014. After years of overdevelopment, when asphalt and trails had compacted soil, damaged tree roots, and disrupted the water flow, threatening the health of the grove, the old roads and trails have been rebuilt, rerouted, or removed to ensure that we will have these trees to wander among and revere for another few thousand years.

Distance: 1.4 miles out and back
Elevation change: 250 feet
Hiking time: 1–2 hours
Trail surface: Boardwalk, paved path, and easy trail
Difficulty: Easy

Maps: The USGS Wawona quad is out of date; follow the maps at the trailhead.
Best time to go: Year-round
Facilities: Restrooms, water, small bookshop, and snacks at the welcome center; restrooms at the trailhead and near the Grizzly Giant

Finding the trailhead: Immediately after entering the park from CA41 at the entrance kiosk, follow the roundabout to the first right turn into the welcome center parking lot. Park and ride the free shuttle bus to the trailhead, about a 10-minute ride. The shuttles run every 5 to 10 minutes. By midmorning they fill up quickly, so you might have to wait a few minutes for the next one. If you arrive before 7 a.m. or after 7 p.m., you can skip the shuttle and drive all the way to the small parking area at the trailhead.

The Hike

The hike described here takes you to the Grizzly Giant and the California Tunnel Tree and back again, but you can study the maps at the trailhead to decide whether you would rather follow the longer Grizzly Giant Loop for a 3.4-mile hike or tackle any one of a number of longer hikes through the grove. It's a place where you can easily spend the whole day.

This and all the trails in the grove are marked by a series of interpretive panels with fascinating tidbits of information about the trees—among them, the fact that these giants have very shallow root systems and very tiny seeds, and that they depend on fire to maintain their health and reproduction.

From the trailhead near the bronze relief map of the grove, follow the boardwalk northeast on a level grade that gradually gives way to packed dirt and begins to climb. At the first junction, take the right fork toward the Grizzly Giant. Cross an old road and climb gently to a beautiful grouping called The Bachelor and the Three Graces at 0.3 mile. The path climbs a bit more steeply now to the massive beheaded Grizzly Giant at 0.6 mile. According to park literature, a single one of the nearly 3,000-year-old tree's lower limbs is larger than the trunk of any non-sequoia here. Other

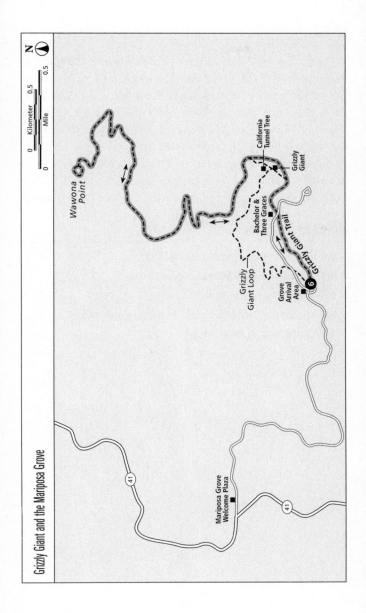

Grizzly Giant and the Mariposa Grove

authorities maintain that it is larger than any other entire tree west of the Mississippi.

Just a few yards beyond the Grizzly Giant is the California Tunnel Tree. The tunnel was cut in 1895 for stagecoaches full of tourists to drive through. Years ago motorists could drive their cars through another of the sequoias here, the Wawona Tunnel Tree, but eventually its roots weakened and the tree fell under an exceptionally heavy snowfall in 1969.

From here you can return the way you came to the trailhead for a total of 1.4 miles or continue on the Grizzly Giant Loop back to the trailhead for a total distance of 3.4 miles.

Miles and Directions

0.0 Start at the Mariposa Grove trailhead.

0.3 Come to The Bachelor and Three Graces.

0.6 Reach the Grizzly Giant.

0.7 Reach the California Tunnel Tree. Retrace your steps.

1.4 Arrive back at the trailhead.

7   Wawona Meadow

Wildflower lovers will find some rare and unusual species blooming along the trail in Wawona Meadow in early season. The shady path beneath a variety of conifers is a favorite stroll in summer, when the temperatures at this low elevation can be uncomfortably hot. This is also one of the few hikes in Yosemite where dogs are allowed.

Distance: 3.5-mile loop
Elevation change: 100 feet
Hiking time: 2–3 hours
Trail surface: Dirt road and smooth trail
Difficulty: Easy
Map: USGS Wawona

Best time to go: Year-round; Apr through June for wildflowers
Facilities: Lodging, store, gas, phones, and restrooms available at Wawona; pit toilet at the trailhead

Finding the trailhead: Drive to the little village of Wawona on the Wawona Road (CA 41). The Wawona Hotel (now Big Trees Lodge) is on the north side of the road, the golf course on the south. Just across from the hotel, a road cuts through the middle of the golf course. On the far side, the parking area and trailhead are marked by a big signboard with photos and information about the area. GPS: N37 32.11' / W119 39.23'

The Hike

You can follow the route in either direction, but it will be described counterclockwise here. The route follows an old, mostly dirt road that's no longer used by vehicles except at the spots where it crosses the Wawona Road.

Start by skirting the south side of the golf course under a cover of incense cedar and ponderosa pine. On the shady forest floor, watch for leafless parasitic plants that live on decaying material in the soil—such as the scarlet snow plant, the knobby brown spikes of pinedrops, and the odd little orchids called coralroot. You can even find lady's slipper orchids in damp hidden patches. In June great clumps of western azalea burst into bloom, along with several kinds of lilies.

The trail leaves the edge of the manicured lawn behind as the meadow begins. This border zone between forest and meadow, called the ecotone, is usually among the richest in living organisms. You might see a cluster of mule deer. They are very tame, but do not attempt to pet or feed them. Mule deer in Yosemite have caused more serious injuries to tourists than have bears.

Now and then a little spur trail leads out into the meadow. There, down among the grasses and sedges, look for little three-petaled white star tulips in May. The tall cabbage-like stalks growing in clumps are the poisonous corn lily. There are islands of willow and chokecherry, usually broadcasting birdsong from warblers and blackbirds. It can be boggy and muddy toward the center, and the vegetation is fragile; step with care.

At 1.7 miles a trail alongside a little creek leads right (east) toward the park's south entrance. Continue along the road and step across another little rivulet. The road becomes partly eroded asphalt and runs through a section of forest in which the bases of the trees are slightly blackened from a management fire.

Cross the Wawona Road at 3.2 miles, just beyond the closed gate. The trail continues on to the Wawona Hotel (Big

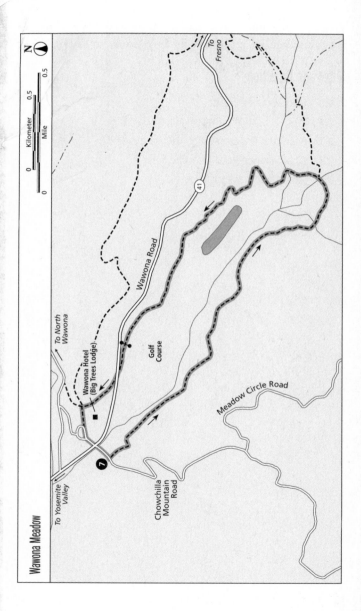

Wawona Meadow

N

Kilometer
0   0.5
0   0.5
Mile

To Fresno

41

Wawona Road

To North Wawona

Wawona Hotel
(Big Trees Lodge)

Golf Course

Meadow Circle Road

7

To Yosemite Valley

Chowchilla Mountain Road

Trees Lodge) where, at 3.4 miles, it crosses the road to the south and cuts back through the golf course to the trailhead.

Miles and Directions

0.0 Start at the trailhead.

1.7 Cross the creek to the trail junction.

3.2 Reach the first crossing of Wawona Road.

3.4 Cross Wawona Road a second time.

3.5 Arrive back at the trailhead.

8 Chilnualna Falls

Chilnualna Creek seldom flows quietly—it rushes and crashes and roars almost constantly for most of its length. One of the most spectacular sections of falling water is just above the point where Chilnualna Creek passes beneath Chilnualna Road and flows into the Merced River. It is as exciting as any of the more famous falls in Yosemite Valley, but few people see it, tucked away as it is in this little corner of the park. This trail takes you so close to the action that you're likely to get soaked from the spray if you go early in the year.

Distance: 0.4 mile out and back
Elevation change: 100 feet
Hiking time: 0.5–1 hour
Trail surface: Rocky forest floor, sometimes steep
Difficulty: Easy

Map: USGS Wawona
Best time to go: Spring through fall; the trail can be icy and dangerous in winter.
Facilities: Pit toilets and bear-proof boxes at the trailhead

Finding the trailhead: From the Wawona Road (CA 41), turn right (east) just beyond Wawona onto Chilnualna Road. Drive 2 miles, passing through the little village of North Wawona, to a signed parking area on the right. GPS: N37 32.53' / W119 38.05'

The Hike

Follow the trail signs from the parking area and cross the road to where a sign routes horse traffic to the left (north), hikers to the right (east). The footpath heads steeply up, sometimes on big granite steps right beside the thundering water. The trailside mosses and ferns are green and lush from the fine

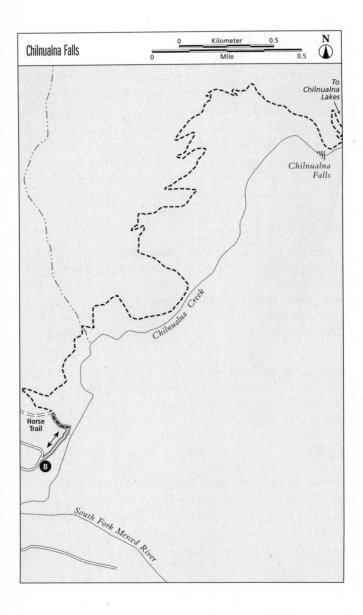

Chilnualna Falls

0 Kilometer 0.5
0 Mile 0.5

N

To Chilnualna Lakes

Chilnualna Falls

Chilnualna Creek

Horse Trail

8

South Fork Merced River

spray. You go no more than 0.2 mile at creekside, but just standing next to all that power is exhilarating.

Do not be tempted to continue scrambling up the slippery and treacherous rocks after the trail cuts left (west), away from the creek. Instead follow the trail to where it meets the horse trail that continues up into the high country.

You can return the way you came, but watch your step on the slick granite. (**Option:** To complete a loop back to the trailhead, follow the horse trail back down along a paved road through a few little vacation homes to the parking area. Doing a loop makes the hike 0.5 mile long.)

Miles and Directions

0.0 Start at the trailhead.

0.2 Reach the lowest of Chilnualna Falls.

0.3 Reach junction with the horse trail.

0.4 Arrive back at the trailhead.

9 Foresta Falls

Foresta Falls is the biggest and most impressive waterfall on Crane Creek, which runs all the way from Crane Flat at 6,200 feet down to the Merced River near El Portal at 2,000 feet in a series of waterfalls and cascades. This is the hike to take early in spring, before the snow has melted from the high country and the valley and the foothills become too hot. This area has suffered several fires over the years, creating perfect conditions for spectacular shows of wildflowers. Local folks know about this waterfall, but very few Yosemite visitors have discovered it.

Distance: 1.8 miles out and back
Elevation change: 300 feet
Hiking time: About 1 hour
Trail surface: Abandoned road
Difficulty: Easy, with some elevation gain

Map: El Portal
Best time to go: Apr through June
Facilities: Food, water, phones, and gas in El Portal

Finding the trailhead: Foresta Road cuts off from CA 120 about 3 miles north of the CA 120/140 junction or about 7 miles south of Crane Flat. Drive 1.7 miles on the paved Foresta Road to an obvious Y junction, marked by a bulletin board where you keep left. In about 2 miles a sign announces that the road is closed ahead. There is no gate blocking the road, but the pavement ends. You can continue on the dirt road for another 50–100 yards to a wide space on the left for two or three cars; park here. The dirt road continues all the way down to the falls, but do not attempt to drive farther; the road becomes impassible, and there is nowhere to turn around. GPS: N37 41.40' / W119 45.36'

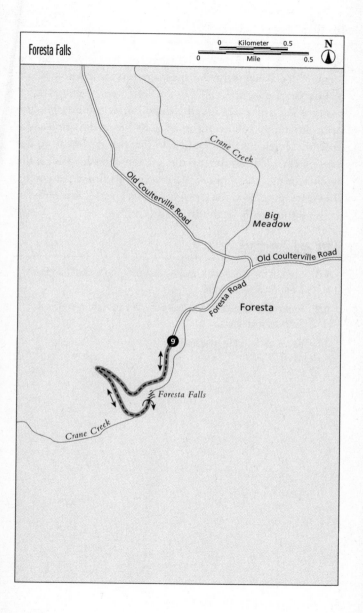

Foresta Falls

0 Kilometer 0.5
0 Mile 0.5

N

Crane Creek

Old Coulterville Road

Big Meadow

Old Coulterville Road

Foresta Road

Foresta

9

Foresta Falls

Crane Creek

The Hike

Your goal is an abandoned bridge over the waterfall on Crane Creek, but from the spot where you leave your car, a short scramble downhill to the left takes you to several pretty pools and cascades, just right for swimming. For the main attraction, follow the road as it heads downhill away from the creek in what looks like the wrong direction, but then makes a hairpin turn to the left and deposits you on the derelict bridge that crosses the creek at its finest viewpoint. Downstream, below the bridge, Crane Creek continues on its tumultuous way to the Merced River.

Miles and Directions

0.0 Start at the small parking area just past the end of the pavement on Foresta Road.

0.9 Reach the derelict bridge over Foresta Falls on Crane Creek. Retrace your steps.

1.8 Arrive back at the trailhead.

Glacier Point Road

M any trails begin along Glacier Point Road, which cuts off from Wawona Road (CA 41) at Chinquapin, a junction about 14 miles from Yosemite Valley at 6,000 feet. The drive itself is beautiful, beginning among ponderosa and sugar pines, climbing through a red fir forest at almost 8,000 feet, then dropping to 7,200 feet at Glacier Point, 16 miles away.

Glacier Point is an extremely popular overlook 3,000 feet above the valley floor. It offers the best views of Half Dome, the valley, and indeed most of the park accessible by road. Almost all the hikes beginning from this road have spectacular views of the valley too. There is a snack bar, gift shop, phones, and toilets, along with an amphitheater for nighttime astronomy programs, and an area from which hang gliders are launched before 8:00 a.m.

The road is open all the way to Glacier Point spring through fall. Bears in the area mean you should not leave ice chests or food in your car. All trailheads have bear-proof boxes for food storage. A hikers' shuttle bus runs daily from the valley during summer. You can get a schedule and fares at the visitor center, or call (209) 372-1240. Reservations are required.

10 Glacier Point

The view from Glacier Point is surely one of the most spectacular in the world. Half Dome occupies center stage, brooding over slickrock Tenaya Canyon and Mirror Lake at the east end of Yosemite Valley. To the right, the Merced River drops into the valley over the Giant Staircase as Nevada and Vernal Falls. Beyond lie rounded Mount Starr King and the darker colored Clark Range. Interpretive panels at the rim help you identify the distant peaks.

Distance: 0.5 mile out and back
Elevation change: Minimal
Hiking time: About 1 hour
Trail surface: Paved, with some packed dirt
Difficulty: Easy
Map: USGS Half Dome
Best time to go: Spring through fall. Glacier Point Road is closed beyond the Yosemite Ski and Snowboard Area in winter, but Glacier Point is a popular destination for experienced cross-country skiers.
Facilities: Food, water, telephones, and restrooms

Finding the trailhead: From the Chinquapin junction on the Wawona Road (CA 41), drive up Glacier Point Road about 16 miles to its end. You can also take a shuttle bus from Yosemite Valley to Glacier Point. GPS: N37 43.39' / W119 34.28'

The Hike

There will be no doubt about which way to go upon leaving the parking lot. Head toward Half Dome, which rears up out of the valley to the north and is backed by granite peaks that stretch to the horizon. About 200 feet past the restrooms there's a big area map to the left (west) of the trail. To the right (southeast) is an amphitheater for nighttime astronomy programs and an area from which hang gliders are launched before 8:00 a.m. on summer mornings. You probably won't notice much of this, though, until you have absorbed some of the stupendous panorama.

Turn left along the path that passes below and in front of an old stone structure containing geologic exhibits about the formation of Yosemite Valley. Glacier Point itself lies slightly downhill and farther to the left (northwest). It is a narrow overhanging platform 7,214 feet above sea level that is bound to look familiar even if this is your first trip to Yosemite. Among the famous photos taken here is that of a group of old-time cancan dancers in mid-kick. Peer over the railing at Curry (Half Dome) Village and the remarkably flat bottom of Yosemite Valley 3,000 feet below, where the Merced River snakes its way from one end to the other. The double waterfall across the way, above Yosemite Lodge, is 2,425-foot Yosemite Falls.

Until 1968 this was the site of the infamous "firefall." The bark of hundreds of magnificent old red firs from the nearby forest was set ablaze just after dark on summer evenings. After an elaborate ceremony of ritual calls between Glacier Point and the valley below, the glowing coals were raked over the cliff to form a fiery waterfall in the dark. It was a popular attraction, but one more suited to an amusement park than to Yosemite. Lichens and other organisms inhabiting the rock face were seared away, and the beautiful old forest was threatened. The National Park Service ended the practice in 1968.

A park ranger is frequently on duty at Glacier Point to answer questions and give short lectures about the history and natural features of the area. Also on duty are innumerable

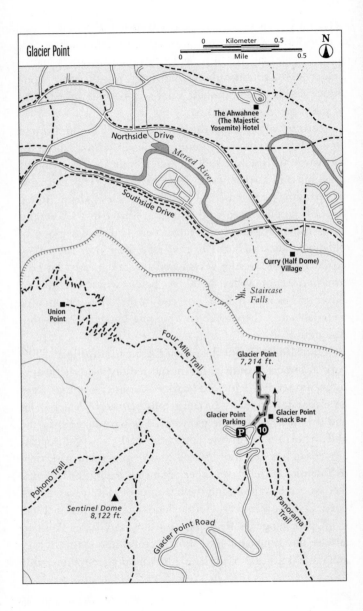

obese, panhandling California ground squirrels. Please do not feed them; this will only encourage their delinquency and further endanger their health.

Miles and Directions

0.0 Start at the trailhead.

0.25 Reach Glacier Point. Retrace your steps.

0.5 Arrive back at the trailhead.

11 Illilouette Fall

This is an upside-down hike to the top of a seldom-seen waterfall and should probably be considered at the very upper limits of an easy day hike, but it isn't difficult if you take your time. Remember that it will take much longer to come back up from the waterfall than it did to go down. Make sure you have allowed plenty of time and that you carry sufficient water.

Distance: 4.2 miles out and back
Elevation change: 1,400 feet
Hiking time: 3–5 hours
Trail surface: Packed earth and forest floor, sometimes rocky
Difficulty: More challenging
Map: USGS Half Dome

Best time to go: Spring and early summer. The trudge back uphill can be hot and dusty later in the season.
Facilities: Snack bar, gift shop, water, restrooms, and telephones at Glacier Point; none at Illilouette Fall

Finding the trailhead: Follow Glacier Point Road to its end 16 miles from Chinquapin on the Wawona Road (CA 41), or take the shuttle from Yosemite Valley to Glacier Point. From the parking lot walk straight toward Half Dome, which looms up out of Yosemite Valley to the northeast. Near the rim of the cliff turn right (east) onto the worn path and look uphill to find the big trailhead sign. GPS: N37 43.39' / W119 34.28'

The Hike

Before you begin, take a minute to enjoy the overwhelming immensity of the panorama at the trailhead. To the left is North Dome, capping the graceful Royal Arches; in the center is Half Dome, the monumental symbol of Yosemite. Tenaya Canyon stretches away to the northeast, and to the west runs the Merced River canyon, down whose Giant Staircase flow Nevada and Vernal Falls. Beautifully sculpted Mount Clark and the Clark Range stretch off to the east.

The only confusing section of the whole route is here at the beginning. Do not immediately strike out along the edge of the cliff to the left (north) of the trail sign. Instead head slightly uphill to the right (south). At 0.1 mile there are two more signs and two trails. To the right (west) is the Pohono Trail, which skirts Yosemite Valley to the west. The Panorama Trail, described here, goes left (south) toward Illilouette Fall.

The first 1.0 mile of the trail switchbacks downward through an area burned in 1987. Fragrant ceanothus and chinquapin, with its spiny green fruits, line the path. This is a good place to listen for the booming call of the sooty grouse in spring and early summer. Males find a territory to their liking then sit and hoot, hour after hour, day after day, hoping to encourage a mate and discourage competitors. Their call is like the sound you make when you blow across the mouth of a glass bottle.

At 1.2 miles a trail coming from Mono Meadow to the south joins the Illilouette Fall Trail. Keep left (northeast) and continue to descend into the Illilouette Gorge. Shrubs give way to forest, and the rush of Illilouette Creek becomes audible. Other hikers have worn a little turnout to the left (north) of the trail to get a look at the falls, just out of sight of the trail itself. This is the only way to see most of Illilouette Fall from any direction because it is tucked so tightly back into the gorge.

Continue to descend a few more switchbacks to reach the footbridge over the creek. The fall is not visible from

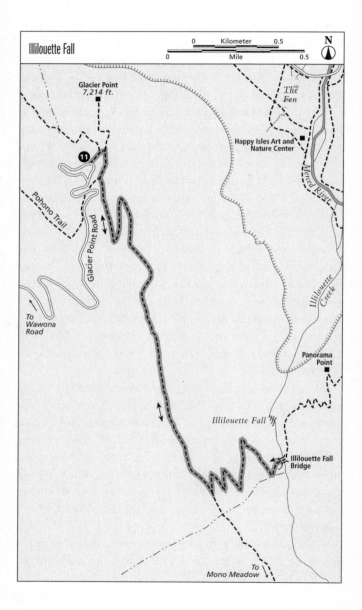

Illilouette Fall

Glacier Point
7,214 ft.

11

Pohono Trail

Glacier Point Road

To Wawona Road

The Fen

Happy Isles Art and Nature Center

Merced River

Illilouette Creek

Panorama Point

Illilouette Fall

Illilouette Fall Bridge

To Mono Meadow

Kilometer
0   0.5
Mile
0   0.5

N

the footbridge, but the creek cascades down in picturesque wedding-cake fashion. In springtime the blooms of western azaleas lining the banks perfume the air.

Return the way you came.

Miles and Directions

0.0 Start at the Panorama/Pohono trailhead.

0.1 Reach the Panorama/Pohono Trail junction.

1.2 Pass the Mono Meadow Trail junction.

2.1 Reach the Illilouette Fall footbridge. Retrace your steps.

4.2 Arrive back at the trailhead.

12 Sentinel Dome

The location of Sentinel Dome above Yosemite Valley provides complete 360-degree views of just about the whole park. Carry water and wear good sturdy shoes for this one; smooth-soled sandals won't give you enough traction on the smooth rock.

Distance: 2.2 miles out and back
Elevation change: 370 feet
Hiking time: 1.5–3 hours
Trail surface: Forest floor and moderately steep slickrock
Difficulty: More challenging

Map: USGS Half Dome
Best time to go: Late spring through fall, whenever the Glacier Point Road is open
Facilities: Pit toilet at the trailhead but no water

Finding the trailhead: From the Wawona Road (CA 41) at Chinquapin, drive 13 miles east up the Glacier Point Road. Parking and the signed trailhead are on the left (northwest). GPS: N37 42.46' / W119 35.12'

The Hike

This dome, like the others in Yosemite, has its origin in the nature of the rock itself. Though the movement of glaciers did not produce it, the scouring action of ice did polish and smooth the rough edges.

Granitic rock forms when molten material under the Earth's crust rises toward the surface but cools and solidifies before it gets there. As the surface material is eroded, pressure on the underlying granite is decreased and the rock expands. The kind of granitic rock that forms Sentinel Dome and others in Yosemite is so solid and massive that it does not break into pieces when it expands. Instead, great sheets of rock pop loose like layers of an onion and are eroded away.

The trail begins at a sign in a sandy opening in the forest that directs you to the right (northeast). The path to the left (west) goes to Taft Point and The Fissures. The rough and rocky path crosses a brook then undulates gradually upward, slowly revealing the top of the dome. Soon the trail curves to the left (north) and proceeds more steeply over smooth and featureless rock. Stenciled metal signs keep you on course.

At 0.4 mile a partly paved service road joins the trail from the right (east). Continue around the base of the dome on your left (west). When you have reached the "back," or more gradually sloping side, of the dome at 0.6 mile, the Pohono Trail splits off to the right (north) and heads down to Glacier Point. Turn left (west) just past this point and head up the steep open slope on an indistinct "path." Don't worry if you lose the track—the only way to go is up. At the dome's summit are the remains of a gnarled Jeffrey pine, once the subject of innumerable photographs and postcards. Dead now and fallen, it is still picturesque.

When you have caught your breath, make a slow circle around the summit. To the northwest, Yosemite Valley, flanked by the Cathedral Rocks on the left (south) and El Capitan on the right (north), stretches toward the coast. If the Great Central Valley is free of smog (a rare occurrence), you can see all the way to the Coast Ranges.

As you move clockwise to the northeast, the entire length of Yosemite Falls comes into view. In early summer you can hear its roar from here. Farther east, the Merced River canyon and Nevada Fall appear and then Mount Clark and the colorful Clark Range, providing a spiky backdrop for the

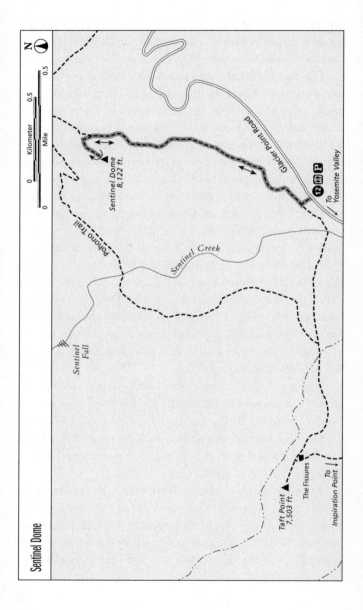

Sentinel Dome

N

Kilometer
0   0.5
0   0.5
Mile

Glacier Point Road

Sentinel Dome
8,122 ft.

Pohono Trail

Sentinel Creek

Sentinel Fall

Taft Point
7,503 ft.

The Fissures

To
Inspiration Point

To Yosemite Valley

12 P

rounded tops of Mount Starr King. The circle is closed by the lower forested country to the south.

When you are ready, return the way you came. Descend very slowly and carefully, avoiding loose sand and gravel whenever possible and taking care to follow the metal signs directing you to the parking lot.

Miles and Directions

0.0 Start at the trailhead.

0.4 Reach the service road.

0.6 Pass the Pohono Trail to Glacier Point.

1.1 Reach the top of Sentinel Dome. Retrace your steps.

2.2 Arrive back at the trailhead.

13 Taft Point and The Fissures

This is an upside-down excursion. After an easy cruise down-hill to Taft Point, you will be climbing up on your way back. Be sure to give yourself plenty of time and take sufficient water with you. Your reward is a striking set of geologic features that will help you understand how Yosemite got its famous profile, with a magnificent—and spine-tingling—view of Yosemite Valley as a bonus.

Distance: 2.2 miles out and back
Elevation change: 250 feet
Hiking time: 2–3 hours
Trail surface: Forest floor and slickrock
Difficulty: Moderate
Map: USGS Half Dome

Best time to go: Spring through fall, when the Glacier Point Road is open
Facilities: Pit toilet at the trailhead but no water; snacks and telephones available at Glacier Point, another 3 miles down the road

Finding the trailhead: From Chinquapin on the Wawona Road (CA 41), turn east onto the Glacier Point Road. Drive 13 miles to the parking area and signed trailhead, which are on the left (west). GPS: N37 42.46' / W119 35.12'

The Hike

The trail begins at a sign in a sandy opening in the mixed pine and fir forest. Follow the path to the left (west) fork. Sentinel Dome lies to the right (north). Pass through a flat, fairly open stretch past an odd, isolated outcrop of almost pure-white quartz on the right, then swing left (south) and start downhill where the forest closes in. At 0.4 mile reach the Pohono Trail junction; continue walking left (west). The trail sign here says you have come only 0.2 mile from the trailhead, but this mileage is out of date.

The forest deepens, and a little creek you will soon cross nourishes a colorful garden of moisture-loving cow parsnip, senecio, corn lily, knotweed, and shooting star. The trail emerges from the shady forest onto open rock and becomes steeper. The flower-filled gully on your right (north) abruptly narrows, deepens, and drops through a notch that sends its little creek plummeting toward the valley floor.

Descend carefully down the rocks past low patches of manzanita and the occasional Jeffrey pine. When the terrain begins to level out, watch for The Fissures on the right. These narrow, deep cracks, or joints, in the granite—up to 40 feet long and slicing inward from the edge of the overhanging cliff—are not visible until you are standing right at their edges. Peering carefully down into one of these cracks, you can see that they cut completely through yards and yards of solid granite, below which there is nothing but about 3,000 feet of thin air between you and the floor of Yosemite Valley. Because of the exposure, this is not a good choice for an evening hike in low light or for a walk with small, unrestrained children.

Once your internal butterflies have settled, proceed toward a slightly rising point with a protective iron railing around it that leans out over the valley like the prow of a ship. This is Taft Point (1.1 miles). Directly across are the Three Brothers, produced by the same jointing process that opened the rock fissures. To the left (west) is the vertical face of El Capitan; to the right (east) is Yosemite Falls. If you stroll westward along the rim, you can see the dramatic knife edges and needlelike spikes of Cathedral Spires.

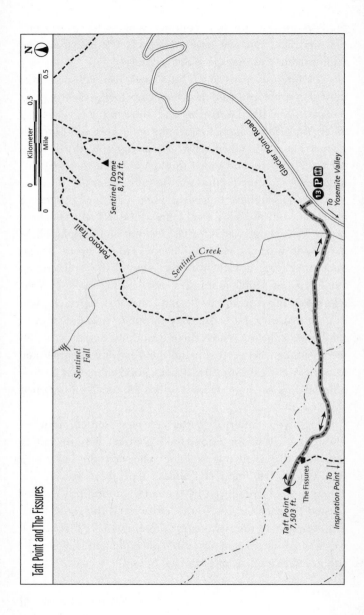

Taft Point and The Fissures

N

Kilometer
0   0.5

Mile
0   0.5

Pohono Trail

Sentinel Dome
8,122 ft.

Sentinel Creek

Sentinel Fall

Glacier Point Road

13 P

To Yosemite Valley

Taft Point
7,503 ft.

The Fissures

To Inspiration Point

When you are ready to return, descend the rise from Taft Point to the first trail sign. (There is a second sign beyond this one. Don't go that far.) The right-hand fork heads south along the Pohono Trail to Inspiration Point. The left (southeast) fork returns to the trailhead and parking area.

Miles and Directions

0.0 Start at the trailhead.

0.4 Reach the Pohono Trail junction.

0.9 Pause at The Fissures.

1.1 Arrive at Taft Point. Retrace your steps.

2.2 Arrive back at the trailhead.

14 McGurk Meadow

This is one of Yosemite's prettiest and "bloomingest" meadows. Most visitors drive right past the unobtrusive trailhead to this little slice of paradise on their way to Glacier Point, so you might be lucky enough to have it all to yourself.

Distance: 1.6 miles out and back
Elevation change: 150 feet
Hiking time: 1–2 hours
Trail surface: Forest floor and slushy meadow

Difficulty: Easy
Maps: USGS El Capitan, Half Dome
Best time to go: All summer; wildflowers best in July
Facilities: None at the trailhead

Finding the trailhead: Drive about 8.5 miles up the Glacier Point Road from the junction with the Wawona Road (CA 41) at Chinquapin. The trailhead is about 200 yards before the entrance to Bridalveil Creek Campground. The campground is on the right (south) side of the road; the trailhead is on the left (north). The signed trailhead itself is about 100 yards beyond (west of) the small parking area and bear-proof boxes. There is nowhere to park near the sign. GPS: N37 40.14' / W119 37.41'

The Hike

The path to the meadow descends through quiet lodgepole pine forest. Currants, strawberries, lupines, larkspur, and many other species flourish alongside the trail.

Just before you reach the meadow at 0.7 mile, watch for a tumbledown log cabin on the left (west). Beyond, at 0.8 mile, lies the meadow. It is threaded by a little brook and spangled with wildflowers of every color: shooting star, lungwort, corn

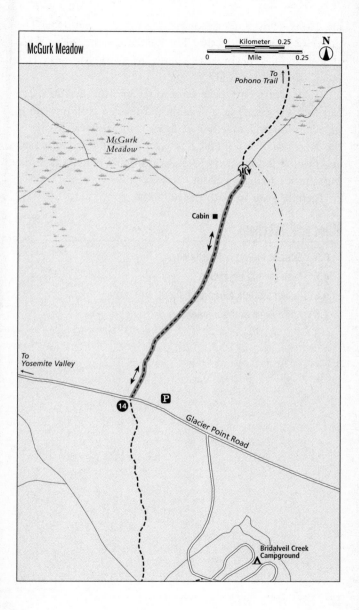

McGurk Meadow

N

0   Kilometer   0.25

0   Mile   0.25

To
Pohono Trail

McGurk
Meadow

Cabin ■

To
Yosemite Valley

14

P

Glacier Point Road

Bridalveil Creek
Campground

lily, monkeyflower, and paintbrush, to name only a few. The meadow is a fairly long one. The flower gardens continue for almost 2 miles, beyond which the McGurk Meadow Trail meets the Pohono Trail.

If you don't care to venture so far into the meadow, you can find a pleasant spot near the footbridge to linger along its edges. Such a meeting of forest and meadow is one of the best places for wildlife watching during the morning and evening hours. Early in the season, that wildlife includes mosquitoes. Bring repellent.

Retrace your steps to the trailhead.

Miles and Directions

0.0   Start at the signed trailhead.

0.7   Pass the old log cabin.

0.8   Reach McGurk Meadow. Retrace your steps.

1.6   Arrive back at the trailhead.

Tioga Road

The Tioga Road (CA 120) is the only automobile route that runs all the way across Yosemite from the Big Oak Flat entrance at 4,800 feet to Tioga Pass at almost 10,000 feet. All the hikes in this section are reached from this road.

There are high peaks, passes, waterfalls, and sensationally beautiful scenery to explore throughout the summer season, but the road is closed once the first winter snowstorms arrive in October or November through the following spring, even June or July, when avalanche danger is mostly past and snow can be cleared. Yosemite is accessible only from the south (CA41) and west (CA 140) sides, and sometimes as far east as Crane Flat on CA 120.

Even in spring and summer, hiking in the higher country may be more challenging when streams are too fast, wide, or high to cross, or bridges or trails are washed out.

15 Tuolumne Grove

The Tuolumne Grove of giant sequoias is not as heavily visited as the Mariposa Grove at the southern end of the park, so you can enjoy the beauty and serenity of walking among the largest living things on Earth in greater solitude here.

Distance: 2.4-mile lollipop
Elevation change: 480 feet
Hiking time: 1–2 hours
Trail surface: Abandoned road
Difficulty: Moderate because of the climb back out
Map: USGS Ackerson Mountain

Best time to go: Spring through fall, whenever the road is open
Facilities: Toilets but no water at the parking lot; gas, groceries, phone, and restrooms at Crane Flat

Finding the trailhead: From Yosemite Valley drive 16 miles north on the Big Oak Flat Road (CA 120) to Crane Flat. Turn right (east) onto the Tioga Road (a continuation of CA 120) and drive less than 1 mile to the Tuolumne Grove parking area on the left (west). The parking lot fills early, but there are more spaces along the road. GPS: N37 45.28' / W119 48.17'

The Hike

The route follows an old road, now closed to vehicle traffic, and passes a life-size model of a cut sequoia stump showing how tree rings indicate the extreme old age of the trees. The road descends through a beautiful old forest where exquisite white dogwoods bloom in springtime among white firs, Douglas firs, sugar pines, and incense cedars. The cedars, with their smooth red bark, are often confused with giant sequoias, but the first of those will not appear for almost a

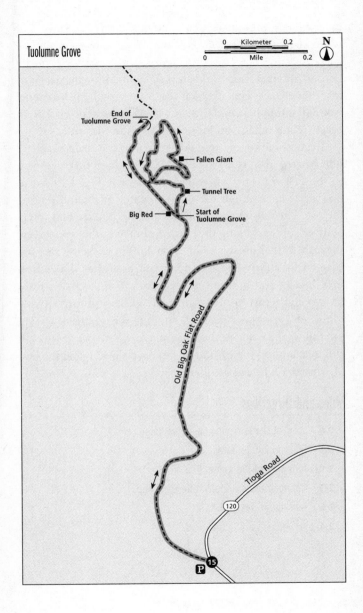

Tuolumne Grove

End of
Tuolumne Grove

Fallen Giant

Tunnel Tree

Big Red

Start of
Tuolumne Grove

Old Big Oak Flat Road

Tioga Road

120

P 15

0   Kilometer   0.2

0   Mile   0.2

N

mile. A sign announces your entrance into the grove, but when the first huge sequoia, "Big Red," shows up on the left, you won't need a sign to tell you have arrived. Shortly beyond, the trail forks and you turn right, following a sign to the Tunnel Tree. This tree was just a stump when the tunnel was cut through it in 1878, but dead or alive, it evokes an eerie feeling when you look straight up from inside.

Beyond the tunnel tree you return to the main road and immediately turn right to begin the short loop that takes you to the Fallen Giant, where little (and some big) kids try to find a passage through the hollow center or scramble along the top. The nature trail loop has a series of excellent interpretive signs explaining the natural history of the trees—how they reach their great ages of up to 3,000 years; how they are adapted to survive repeated fires; and how they depend on fires, insects, and squirrels to reproduce. Cross a little stream or two and return to the main trail, where you turn sharply to the left (south) to hike back uphill to the trailhead. Or you can follow the road another 0.5 mile to where the grove ends and turn around there, though you have already seen the best of what the hike has to offer.

Miles and Directions

0.0 Start at the Tuolumne Grove trailhead.

0.9 Enter Tuolumne Grove.

1.0 Turn right to the Tunnel Tree.

1.1 Continue around the Nature Trail Loop.

1.5 Turn left at the main trail.

2.4 Arrive back at the trailhead.

16 May Lake

May Lake High Sierra Camp is one of five popular back-country camps with tent cabins and other amenities that are available to visitors by reservation only. You can hike in to spend the day with little effort, since it is the nearest of all the camps to a road (not counting Tuolumne Meadows Lodge). Mount Hoffman, at the geographical center of Yosemite, provides the backdrop to this idyllic lake.

Distance: 2.4 miles out and back
Elevation change: 500 feet
Hiking time: 2–4 hours
Trail surface: Rocky forest floor and switchbacks
Difficulty: Moderate
Map: USGS Tenaya Lake

Best time to go: All summer, whenever the Tioga Road is open and free of snow
Facilities: Toilets but no water at the trailhead; toilets and water at May Lake. Please use the toilets at the campground, not at the High Sierra Camp. A small store at the High Sierra Camp is open for a few hours each day.

Finding the trailhead: The May Lake Road junction lies along the Tioga Road (CA 120) 27 miles east of Crane Flat and 20 miles west of Tioga Pass. Follow the narrow road north about 2 miles to the trailhead. Drive with care. In many places the road is only wide enough for one vehicle at a time. Leave any food or ice chests in the bear-proof boxes at the trailhead. GPS: N37 49.57' / W119 29.28'

The Hike

The hike begins in a shady glen with a variety of conifers—lodgepole and silver pine, hemlock, and fir—and passes a

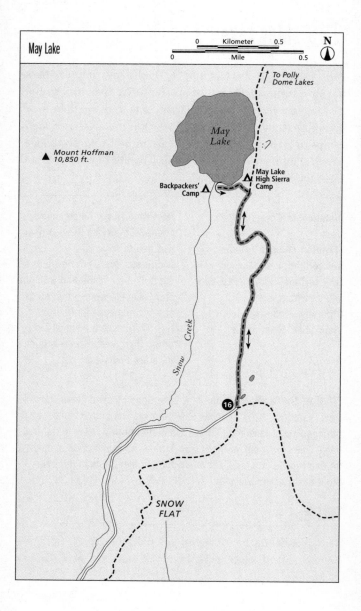

little brown pond teeming with fairy shrimp and other interesting creatures. The well-used trail climbs slowly at first, passing through granite corridors where cracks bloom with ferns, mountain pride penstemon, shaggy hawkweed, and other wildflowers.

The trail ascends gradually then begins a steeper, winding climb. There are good views now and then down Tenaya Canyon past Clouds Rest and Half Dome. The dramatic pointy peak in the distance is Mount Clark. Back up the canyon to the right (southeast), you can just glimpse Tenaya Lake.

The trail flattens out in forest and in just a few yards reaches a trail fork at May Lake at 1.2 miles. To the left (west) is the camping area; to the right (east) is the High Sierra Camp, marked by a row of white tent cabins. There is a backpacker campground nearby.

Enjoy the lakeshore, but do not jump in. This is the local water supply, and swimming is prohibited. Mount Hoffman (10,850 feet) rises dramatically behind the lake to the west.

Miles and Directions

0.0 Start at the trailhead.

1.2 Reach May Lake. Retrace your steps.

2.4 Arrive back at the trailhead.

17 Tenaya Lake

Tenaya Lake was named for Chief Tenaya, who, with all his people, was driven from his home in Yosemite by the US Cavalry. It is a very big lake by Yosemite standards—a very popular one too, with its wide sandy beach and proximity to the road. This hike takes you around the quiet "back" side of the lake, away from the busy highway.

Distance: 0.4 mile out and back
Elevation change: Negligible
Hiking time: 1–2 hours
Trail surface: Mostly forest floor, some paved surface
Difficulty: Easy
Map: USGS Tenaya Lake (*Note:* The topo map is out of date and incorrect.)

Best time to go: All summer, whenever Tioga Road is open (though crossing the inlet at high water may be hazardous early in the season).
Facilities: Toilets and bear-proof boxes at the trailhead

Finding the trailhead: Ride the free shuttle bus from Tuolumne Meadows to Stop 9 at the northeast end of Tenaya Lake, or drive to the same spot on the Tioga Road (CA 120). Turn southeast into the trailhead parking lot, where there are bear-proof boxes, toilets, and a big up-to-date trail map. GPS: N37 50.16' / W119 27.08'

The Hike

Follow the boardwalk and a short section of paved trail that takes you across a slushy area through lodgepole pine forest. The ground cover beneath the pines is Sierra bilberry which, like its cousin the blueberry, has edible fruit and turns red in the fall. There are several very informative interpretive signs

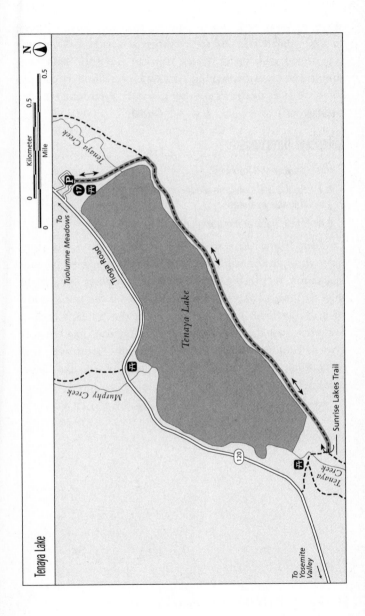

Tenaya Lake

along the way, well worth pausing to read. Cross a bridge to find yourself on the sandy shore of Tenaya Lake, which is scattered with picnic tables. You can end your walk here, sunning, wading, picnicking, and watching climbers cling to the rock faces of the surrounding domes, then return to the parking area.

Miles and Directions

0.0 Start at the trailhead.

0.2 Reach the Tuolumne Meadows/Sunrise Lakes junction. Retrace your steps.

0.4 Arrive back at the trailhead.

Option: If you want to explore further, walk a few paces more through the sand, carefully avoiding roped-off lakeside vegetation recovering from years of trampling. Reach the inlet to Tenaya Lake. You can wade across if the water is low or look upstream for a log crossing if the water is high. A few yards past the inlet, reach a trail junction. The left fork goes to Tuolumne Meadows. Take the right (southwest) fork to continue along the lakeshore as long as you like before turning back.

18 Lukens Lake

This easy and popular hike through forest and meadow to a quiet lake is a favorite with wildflower lovers.

Distance: 2.0 miles out and back
Elevation change: 150 feet
Hiking time: 1-2 hours
Trail surface: Forest floor and slushy meadow
Difficulty: Easy

Map: USGS Yosemite Falls (**Note:** This topo is out of date and incorrect.)
Best time to go: All summer, whenever the Tioga Road is open; wildflowers best in July
Facilities: None at the trailhead

Finding the trailhead: Drive on the Tioga Road (CA 120) about 2 miles east of the White Wolf junction. The signed parking area is on the south side of the road; the trail begins on the north side. GPS: N37 51.04' / W119 36.53'

The Hike

To begin this hike, carefully cross the Tioga Road and head uphill through an almost pure red fir forest. The cones underfoot come from the occasional western white pine or hemlock. Fir cones do not fall—they decompose and release their seeds while still on the tree. Watch for odd, leafless plants like pinedrops, brilliant red snow plant, and little coral-root orchids on the forest floor. Because these species have no green leaves and thus cannot make food for themselves through photosynthesis, they live on decaying material in the soil. Chinquapin—green-and-gold shrubs with spiny but delicious edible nuts—grow in the sunny spots.

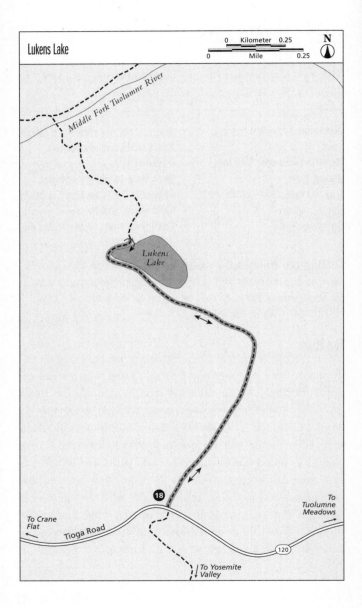

The trail tops a rise and then descends to a creek filled with dozens of species of waist-high wildflowers like the tall white cow parsnip, blue lupine, yellow senecio, and dozens more. The trail turns left (northwest) and follows the forest edge alongside a meadow, then skirts the lake. The showy white shrubs along the shore are Labrador tea, a close relative of azaleas and blueberries.

Hop the outlet stream at the end of the lake and follow the shore a few yards around the north end, where there are plenty of inviting shady picnic spots. (Camping is prohibited.) The lake is shallow, grassy, and muddy around the edges—not the best choice for a swim. Early in the year, the moisture that nourishes the wildflowers means there will be mosquitoes. Take repellent.

Retrace your steps to the Tioga Road.

Miles and Directions

0.0 Start at the trailhead.

0.8 Reach and follow the creek.

1.0 Arrive at Lukens Lake. Retrace your steps.

2.0 Arrive back at the trailhead.

Tuolumne Meadows

At an elevation of 8,600 feet, the Tuolumne Meadows region is the only developed area (summer only) on the eastern side of the park, about 8 miles from Tioga Pass. There is a campground, visitor center, store, cafe, and the Tuolumne Meadows Lodge (tent cabins only). There is no gas at Tuolumne Meadows; the nearest station is at Crane Flat, back to the west, or at Lee Vining, east of the park entrance on US 395. (Driving the Tioga Road between Tioga Pass and Lee Vining down on US 395 is an adventure in itself, especially if you have never done it.)

A shuttle bus runs between Tuolumne Lodge and Olmstead Point every hour. The Tuolumne Meadows hikers' bus leaves Yosemite Valley and makes several stops on the way to Tuolumne Meadows Lodge every day. There is a charge depending upon where you want to be dropped off. A schedule and map of shuttle stops is available at the visitor center.

19 Dog Lake

A moderately steep but shady uphill climb takes you to the shore of this pretty little lake tucked in behind Lembert Dome. It's worthwhile anytime, but photography is best in the afternoon.

Distance: 2.6 miles out and back
Elevation change: 600 feet
Hiking time: 2–3 hours
Trail surface: Rocky packed earth
Difficulty: Moderate
Map: USGS Tioga Pass

Best time to go: Late spring to fall, whenever the Tioga Road is open
Facilities: Picnic tables and toilets at the trailhead but no potable water; supplies, telephone, and groceries available at the Tuolumne Meadows store, about 0.5 mile west on the Tioga Road

Finding the trailhead: From the west, follow the Tioga Road (CA 120) eastward past the Tuolumne Meadows Visitor Center, store, and campground, all on the right (south) side of the road. About 100 yards beyond the bridge over the Tuolumne River, turn left (north) into the Lembert Dome parking area.

From the east (Tioga Pass), follow the Tioga Road past the turnoff to the Wilderness Center on the left (south). The sign for the center reads "Wilderness Permits, Pacific Crest, John Muir." About 100 yards beyond the sign, turn right (north) into the Lembert Dome lot. GPS: N37 52.38' / W119 21.13'

The Hike

Set out northward from the small Lembert Dome/Dog Lake trailhead sign through lodgepole pines. Cross an open rocky slab polished to a high sheen in places by glaciers and reenter the forest. Sometimes there are cairns to guide you, but sometimes they get washed away. Just walk straight across the rocks and watch for the continuation of the trail on the far side (north). At 0.1 mile a trail comes in from the stables to the left (west). Take the right (north) fork. Just beyond, another trail comes in from the stables. Keep right (north) again. Climb steeply alongside the sheer face of Lembert Dome and then cross a little creek. The grade now becomes less extreme.

At 1.0 mile reach a three-way junction where you keep left toward Dog Lake and Young Lakes (northeast). The right fork goes around the back of Lembert Dome. Don't let the trail sign here confuse you on your way back. The Dog Lake trailhead noted on this sign is not the one you came in on and will not take you back to where you started. You started at the Lembert Dome parking area. At mile 1.2 you reach another junction. The left fork goes to Young Lakes (north); your trail goes right (northwest). In only 0.1 mile more you reach an opening in the forest that perfectly frames Dog Lake.

The lake is surrounded on three sides by lodgepole pines, but at the far east end a green (or golden, depending on the season) meadow provides the foreground for the huge red bulks of Mount Dana and Mount Gibbs.

Camping is not permitted here, tempting as it may be. The area is too delicate and too close to the busy road and would be trampled in no time. It is possible to circumnavigate the lake via a use trail, but it's muddy and the lakeside vegetation is fragile. Enjoy the view from the lake's west end, then return the way you came.

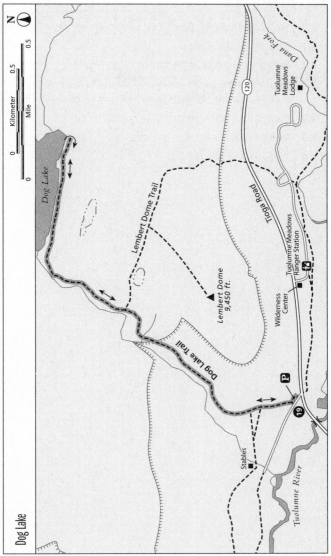

Dog Lake

Miles and Directions

0.0 Start at the Lembert Dome/Dog Lake trailhead.

0.1 Pass trail to the stables.

0.2 Pass a second trail to the stables.

1.0 Keep left at the junction, heading toward Dog Lake and Young Lakes. The Lembert Dome trail goes right.

1.2 Come to the Dog Lake cutoff. Keep right.

1.3 Reach Dog Lake. Retrace your steps.

2.6 Arrive back at the trailhead.

20 Lembert Dome

Lembert Dome—among the premier features of Tuolumne Meadows—is the huge, lopsided, smoothly polished mound of granite just north of the Tioga Road. This loop will take you all the way around the dome, providing some great views along the way. There are even better views from the top, of course, but the route is strenuous and slippery and far beyond the definition of an "easy" hike. You can follow the route in either direction, but it will be described clockwise here.

Distance: 3.1-mile loop
Elevation change: 500 feet
Hiking time: 2–3 hours
Trail surface: Packed forest floor, sometimes rocky
Difficulty: Moderate
Map: USGS Tioga Pass

Best time to go: Late June through mid-Sept, when the Tioga Road is open
Facilities: Picnic tables and toilets at the trailhead but no potable water; supplies, telephone, and groceries available at the Tuolumne Meadows store, about 0.5 mile west on the Tioga Road

Finding the trailhead: From the west follow the Tioga Road (CA 120) past the Tuolumne Meadows Visitor Center, store, cafe, and campground, all on the right (south) side of the road. About 150 yards beyond the bridge over the Tuolumne River, turn left (north) into the Lembert Dome parking area.

From the east (Tioga Pass) follow the Tioga Road past the turnoff to the Wilderness Center on the left (south) side of the road. Continue for about 100 yards and turn right (north) into the Lembert Dome parking area. GPS: N37 52.38' / W119 21.13'

The Hike

Set out northward from the trailhead, past the picnic tables and restrooms from the Lembert Dome/Dog Lake trailhead sign. Pass beneath lodgepole pines and then cross an open, rocky slab where the route is marked by big boulders. Glaciers polished the granite to a high sheen in patches. If you look carefully, you can see striations or scratches in the rock that show the direction in which the rivers of ice flowed.

At 0.2 mile a trail comes in from the stables to the left (west). Take the right (north) fork. Just beyond, another trail comes in from the same direction. Keep right (north) again.

Climb alongside the sheer face of Lembert Dome, then cross a little creek. The grade becomes more gradual. At 1.1 miles turn right (east) at the signed junction. The left fork goes north and uphill to Dog Lake. Saunter along an almost flat path, passing a little pond at the base of the dome.

At 1.7 miles reach another junction, not shown on the topo map; this one leads to the top of Lembert Dome. Your trail continues downhill to the left (south). Follow the steep switchbacks downhill to the Tioga Road. Cross the road at 2.5 miles; continue 0.1 mile to the parking lot on a small side road that leads to Tuolumne Meadows Lodge. Cross the road to the south and find a trail sign marking the John Muir Trail at 2.6 miles. Turn right (west) and follow the John Muir Trail alongside the Tioga Road to where you can cross the road at the Lembert Dome parking area.

Miles and Directions

0.0 Start at the Lembert Dome/Dog Lake trailhead.

0.2 Pass the trails from the stables.

1.3 Reach the Lembert Dome/Dog Lake trail junction.

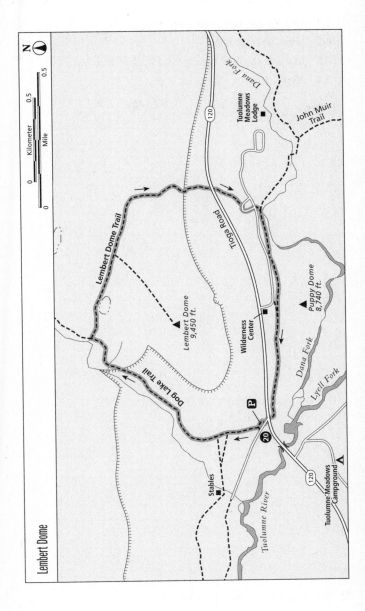

1.7 Pass the trail to the top of the dome.

2.5 Cross the Tioga Road.

2.6 Turn right (west) at the sign onto the John Muir Trail.

3.1 Arrive back at the trailhead.

21 Pothole Dome

Pothole Dome looks like a much smaller version of Lembert Dome at the other end of Tuolumne Meadows. Interesting glacial features and great views make it such a popular hike that the vegetation between the road and the dome is in danger of becoming trampled. Please stay on the trail.

Distance: 1.0 mile out and back
Elevation change: 200 feet
Hiking time: 0.5-1 hour
Trail surface: Grassy meadow and slickrock

Difficulty: Easy
Map: USGS Falls Ridge
Best time to go: All summer, whenever the Tioga Road is open
Facilities: None at the trailhead

Finding the trailhead: Following the Tioga Road (CA 120), drive or ride the Tuolumne Meadows shuttle about 1.5 miles west of the visitor center. The parking area and trailhead are on the right (north) side of the road. There are several signs, including an interpretive panel about life in the meadow. GPS: N37 52.38' / W119 23.46'

The Hike

The trail skirts the meadow to the west and crosses over to the dome along the edge of the forest. It then swings right (east), back toward the low end of the dome, describing a wide U. Skirt the edge of the dome until you reach a convenient place to start up the long, smooth slope to its summit.

Here you will find a number of fine examples of glacial activity. There are patches of glacial polish—rock surfaces buffed to an almost blinding sheen by the movement of fine grit dragged across the rock by moving ice. Huge boulders improbably perched on top of the dome were deposited

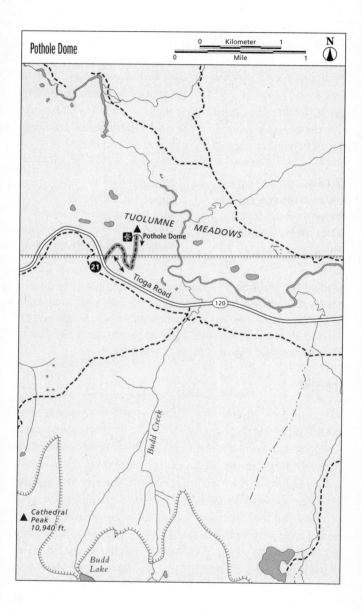

Pothole Dome

TUOLUMNE MEADOWS

Pothole Dome

21

Tioga Road

120

Budd Creek

Cathedral
Peak
10,940 ft.

Budd
Lake

N

0   Kilometer   1

0   Mile   1

there by the glaciers. Here and there are the potholes for which the dome was named, hollowed out by swirling water trapped beneath the glacial ice.

Enjoy the spectacular 360-degree view from the top, which includes the northern boundary country of the park; Mount Gibbs, Mount Dana, and Lembert Dome to the east; and the Cathedral Range to the south. Return, slowly and carefully, to the trailhead using the same trail.

Miles and Directions

0.0 Start at the trailhead.

0.5 Reach the summit of Pothole Dome. Carefully retrace your steps.

1.0 Arrive back at the trailhead.

22 Soda Springs and Parsons Lodge

A wide, sandy trail heads right into the heart of enormous Tuolumne Meadows amid a riot of wildflowers and crosses the Tuolumne River as it winds its sinuous way through the meadow. Beyond, you can visit mysterious Soda Springs and stop at historic Parsons Lodge, which houses exhibits of early days in Yosemite.

Distance: 1.2 miles out and back
Elevation change: 40 feet
Hiking time: 1–2 hours
Trail surface: Packed earth and gravel road
Difficulty: Easy

Maps: USGS Tioga Pass, Vogelsang Peak
Best time to go: All summer, whenever the Tioga Road is open
Facilities: Food, water, gas, post office, and telephone available nearby in Tuolumne Meadows village

Finding the trailhead: From the visitor center in Tuolumne Meadows, drive about 150 yards east on the Tioga Road (CA 120) to the signed trailhead on the left (north) side of the road. GPS: N37 52.20' / W119 22.13'

The Hike

The trail begins amid an expanse of wildflowers such as purple meadow penstemon and shooting stars, white pussytoes, and yellow goldenrod. The Tuolumne River lies ahead, and off to the right (east) is long, sloping Lembert Dome. Farther beyond rise the two red bulks of Mounts Dana and Gibbs. To their right is gray-granite Mammoth Peak.

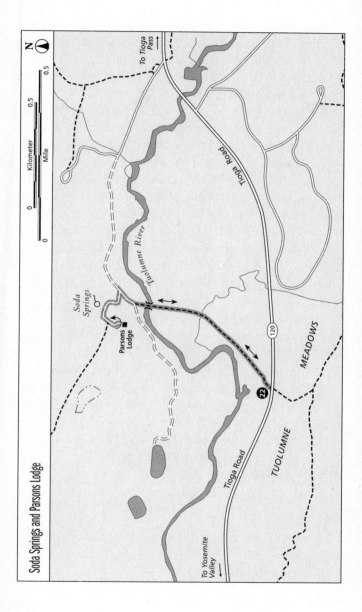

Soda Springs and Parsons Lodge

At the main channel of the river, the path crosses a wood-and-stone footbridge. Pause here and turn around for a panoramic view of the Cathedral Range to the south. The spires of Cathedral Peak itself, Echo Peak, and the Cockscomb rise behind smoothly rounded Fairview Dome.

Just beyond the bridge, the trail intersects a gravel road at 0.4 mile. Turn left (west) here; proceed about 50 yards to another sign directing you right (north) and up a little slope to Soda Springs and Parsons Lodge (0.6 mile).

Parsons Lodge, built of local stone by the Sierra Club in 1915 and sold to the National Park Service in 1973, is open daily during summer and contains exhibits on the history of the area. Next door, the log-built McCauley Cabin houses park service volunteers, who are eager to share information about the area. Rest for a while on the rocks in front of the lodge to watch the activities of the marmot families that live in burrows nearby.

From the lodge head toward the tumbledown, roofless log structure clearly visible to the east. Here naturally carbonated Soda Springs bubbles out of the ground in dozens of places, staining the soil red-brown. It's a good place to see mule deer, which come to lick the minerals deposited by the springs. You can spend a whole day wandering these meadows, using the well-marked trails to create your own loop, or you can return the way you came to the Tioga Road.

Miles and Directions

0.0 Start at the trailhead.

0.4 Reach the gravel road.

0.6 Arrive at Parsons Lodge. Retrace your steps. (**Option:** Create a loop with additional meadows trails.)

1.2 Arrive back at the trailhead.

23 Dana Fork Cascades

This short section of the Dana Fork of the Tuolumne River is within minutes of a major trailhead and just a few steps off the John Muir Trail, but most hikers seem to miss it. There are usually a few anglers and picnickers but this spot never seems to draw the crowds it deserves, partly because it's half-way hidden.

The rock of the stream bed has been carved and smoothed in such intricate curves and hollows, such perfectly round potholes and wavy elongated troughs and unexpected patterns that you could be standing at the edge of an oversized Henry Moore sculpture. The dry stream bed alone would be a work of art, but at high water the beautiful shapes are still visible and become softer and even more interesting. In spring and early summer the river runs down a number of stairsteps of different widths, and at the upper end of the cascades makes a pretty little waterfall. Once you have discovered it, it's a hard place to leave.

Distance: 0.4 mile out and back
Hiking time: 20 minutes
Elevation change: Minimal
Difficulty: Easy
Seasons: Spring and summer, whenever the Tioga Road is open

Nearest facilities: Tuolumne Village
Permit: None
Maps: Vogelsang Peak and Tioga Pass, but not really needed

Finding the trailhead: From the west drive Tioga Road (CA 120) eastward past the Tuolumne Meadows visitor center, store, and campground, all on the right. Cross the bridge over the Tuolumne River and in a mile turn right at the entrance to the Wilderness Center. Follow

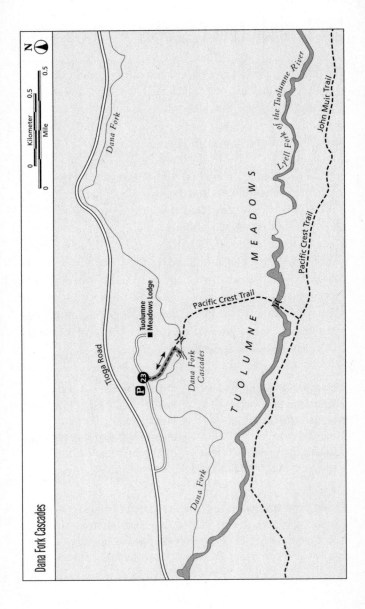

the road as it curves around to the left for about a half mile to the Dog Lake parking lot on the left.

The Hike

From the Dog Lake parking lot, cross the road and walk a few yards downhill to meet the John Muir Trail where you turn left (east). You will scarcely notice the Dana Fork of the Tuolumne River flowing fairly quietly alongside on your right at first. Then, after a few yards, an outcrop of granite comes between you and the river at the same time that you begin to hear the noisy splashing that indicates some boisterous water activity. Turn off the trail and make your way around or (carefully) over the rocks that hide the stream, and join the very anglers and photographers who have discovered it. Return the way you came.

Miles and Directions

0.0 Start at the Dog Lake parking lot.

0.1 John Muir Trail, turn left.

0.2 View of the river is blocked by granite outcropping, scramble over this or go around.

0.4 Return to the trailhead.

24 Lyell Fork

This route is part of the famous John Muir Trail and the Pacific Crest Trail. It follows the Tuolumne River to a set of bridges at the foot of a grand meadow, one of the prettiest places in the park. You will probably want to spend hours there, so allow plenty of time.

Distance: 1.2 miles out and back
Elevation change: 60 feet
Hiking time: 0.5–1 hour
Trail surface: Rocky packed earth through forest
Difficulty: Easy

Maps: USGS Tioga Pass, Vogelsang Peak
Best time to go: All summer, whenever the Tioga Road is open
Facilities: None at the trailhead; food, phones, gas, water, and restrooms available less than 1 mile west on the Tioga Road

Finding the trailhead: From the west, follow the Tioga Road (CA 120) eastward past the Tuolumne Meadows Visitor Center, store, and campground, all on the right (south) side of the road. Cross the bridge over the Tuolumne River. About 0.5 mile beyond the bridge, turn right (south) at the entrance to the Wilderness Center and follow the road as it curves left (east) for 0.5 mile to the Dog Lake parking lot on the left (north). Store any food or ice chests in the bear-proof boxes provided. Do not leave anything that looks or smells like food in your car. This parking lot fills up quickly; the earlier you arrive, the better your chances of finding a parking space. GPS: N37 52.33' / W119 20.07'

The Hike

Cross the road south of the parking lot to the trailhead sign. The trail rambles alongside the Dana Fork of the Tuolumne

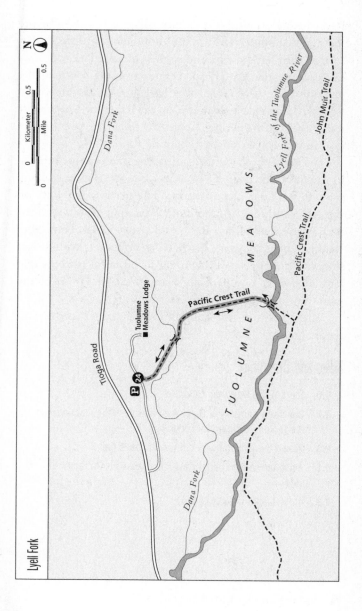

Lyell Fork

River before crossing it on a footbridge at 0.2 mile. Ignore the sign that points north to the Tuolumne Meadows Lodge. Instead turn left (east) just after the crossing. The trail continues along the Dana Fork before swinging south to the junction with the Gaylor Lakes Trail at 0.3 mile. Keep right (south), then pass a marshy area on the left (east). Cross a low rocky rise and turn right (south) to reach the two bridges over the Lyell Fork of the Tuolumne River.

The scene from the bridges is one of the most sublime in Yosemite. The river is a brilliant turquoise ribbon winding through the long, green meadow. The massive gray hulk on the left (southeast) is Mammoth Peak (not to be confused with Mammoth Mountain, the ski resort, which lies farther south). Where the river reaches the bridges, it rushes over smoothly rounded rocks, swirling in beautiful patterns that have hollowed out perfectly round shallow bowls in the granite before tumbling into clear pools.

When you can tear yourself away, retrace your steps to the trailhead.

Miles and Directions

0.0 Start at the Dog Lake trailhead.

0.2 Cross the bridge over Dana Fork and pass the junction with the Tuolumne Meadows Lodge Trail.

0.3 Reach the junction with the Gaylor Lakes Trail.

0.6 Arrive at the twin bridges over the Lyell Fork. Retrace your steps.

1.2 Arrive back at the trailhead.

Hetch Hetchy

Hetch Hetchy Reservoir, completed in 1923 and expanded in 1938, provides water and power for the City of San Francisco. Before the O'Shaughnessy Dam captured and tamed the Tuolumne River, the Hetch Hetchy Valley was said to rival Yosemite in scenic beauty. John Muir's famous, if fruitless, battle against the dam brought the need to preserve such wilderness treasures to the attention of the American public and gave impetus to the growth of the National Park Service and to the conservation movement as a whole.

The area around the lake has the best display of springtime wildflowers in the park. It's a great place to hike in early season, when the higher country is still under snow; and it's pleasant in October, when the black oaks change color. In midsummer it's dry and hot. No swimming or boating is allowed in the reservoir.

To reach the main Hetch Hetchy trailhead at the O'Shaughnessy Dam, you must leave Yosemite National Park at the Big Oak Flat entrance station (if you are coming from the east) and reenter the park at the Hetch Hetchy entrance station, about 8 miles up Evergreen Road. From the west, turn off the highway before you reach the main (Big Oak Flat) entrance station. Ask about the condition of the road before you start out—it washes out regularly and may be closed for repairs.

Note: Because the reservoir is a crucial source of water and power for San Francisco, park rangers at the entrance kiosk will hand you a numbered tag for your dashboard or mirror that you must return on your way out. You cannot spend the night at Hetch Hetchy unless you have a backpackers' wilderness permit, which gives you permission to stay one night at the backpackers' campground.

25 Tueeulala and Wapama Falls

The area around the Hetch Hetchy Reservoir has the best springtime wildflower display in the park, and it's a good place for a hike when the higher country is still under snow. In springtime, snowmelt water pours over Wapama Falls with tremendous force. By midsummer the falls are dry and the hike can be uncomfortably hot, but in October the leaves of the black oaks turn bright yellow and the temperature cools. The area is recovering from the 2013 Rim Fire, but the hike is still beautiful. There are patches of blackened foliage on the cliffs above the trail and some singed spots near the lakeside, but the spring wildflowers, always spectacular here, are especially abundant after fire has enriched the soil and cleared away some of the shrubbery.

Distance: 5.0 miles out and back
Elevation change: 200 feet
Hiking time: 3–4 hours
Trail surface: Abandoned road, rocky trail
Difficulty: More challenging
Map: USGS Lake Eleanor

Best time to go: Mid-Apr to June (hot and dry later in summer); Oct for foliage
Facilities: Water, restrooms, and phone on the right side of the road just before the dam and the parking area on the one-way loop road

Finding the trailhead: Drive 1 mile west of the Big Oak Flat entrance station to Yosemite National Park on CA 120. Turn right (north) onto Evergreen Road and drive about 7 miles. At Camp Mather turn right (northeast) onto Hetch Hetchy Road. After about 1 mile, pass through the park entrance station, where you will be given a day-use permit for your dashboard and your vehicle license number will be registered. These precautions have been in effect since the 9/11 terrorist attacks, as Hetch Hetchy Reservoir contains the water supply for the City of San Francisco. Continue for 8 miles to where the road ends in a one-way loop. The parking area is partway around the loop and just beyond the dam. GPS: N37 56.35' / W119 47.15'

The Hike

Hetch Hetchy Reservoir—built between 1914 and 1923 and expanded in 1938—provides water and power for the City of San Francisco, so no swimming or boating is allowed.

To begin the hike, walk across the dam past some historical markers and colorful interpretive panels about the benefits of the dam installed by the City of San Francisco. On the far side, at 0.1 mile, enjoy the troupe of acrobatic swallows swooping and diving before the entrance to a dark and dripping tunnel. Pass through the tunnel and continue along the level road skirting the lake.

The roadside is lined with live oak, bay trees, and poison oak, along with dozens of species of wildflowers, including showy pink-and-yellow harlequin lupines. The low elevation here makes this a likely spot for encounters with snakes of several kinds, including rattlers. They are not aggressive, but they should be avoided. If you're lucky you'll catch the spring migration of millions of little brown-and-orange California newts. Water trickles down cracks in the rock to nourish buttercups, monkeyflowers, and columbines.

The road climbs slowly for a while, then at 0.9 mile the trail to the falls leaves the road and turns right (east). The left (north) route leads to Lake Vernon. The Wapama Falls Trail rises and falls and curves back and forth among more delicate little gardens, waterfalls, and pools, while Kolana Rock broods darkly over the reservoir on the other side.

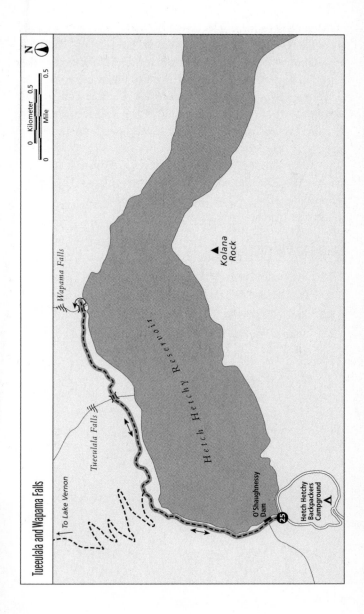

Tueeulala and Wapama Falls

To Lake Vernon

Tueeulala Falls

Wapama Falls

Hetch Hetchy Reservoir

Kolana Rock

O'Shaughnessy Dam

25

Hetch Hetchy Backpackers Campground

N

0   Kilometer   0.5
0   Mile   0.5

Tueeulala Falls tumbles down over the trail, so you might get your feet wet early in the season, but by June the little waterfall may be dry. Continue along the cliff above the lake, climbing and descending for 1.5 miles more until you can feel the spray and hear the thunder of Wapama Falls ahead. Toward the bottom, the falls split into several sections, each of which is crossed on a separate footbridge. Sometimes the bridges are underwater shin-deep, though safe to wade; at other times the force of the torrent is so great that it is not safe to cross. You can enjoy the falls from either side or from the middle—if you crave a refreshing shower.

Return the way you came.

Miles and Directions

0.0 Start at the Hetch Hetchy trailhead.

0.1 Pass through the tunnel.

0.9 Reach the Lake Vernon Trail junction.

2.5 Arrive at Wapama Falls. Retrace your steps.

5.0 Arrive back at the trailhead.

About the Author

Suzanne Swedo, director of W.I.L.D. (wildswedo.com), has backpacked the mountains of every continent. She has led groups into the wilderness for more than thirty years and teaches wilderness survival and natural sciences for individuals, schools, universities, museums, and organizations such as the Yosemite Conservancy and the Sierra Club. She is author of *Wilderness Survival, Hiking Yosemite National Park, Hiking California's Golden Trout Wilderness,* and *Hiking the Hawaiian Islands* for FalconGuides. She lectures and consults about backpacking, botany, and survival on radio and television as well as in print.